THE
POWER
OF
KNOWLEDGE

A BOOK OF THE
NEW MESSAGE
FROM GOD

THE
POWER
OF
KNOWLEDGE

The
GREATER INTELLIGENCE
within You

AS REVEALED TO
Marshall Vian Summers

THE
POWER
OF
KNOWLEDGE

Copyright © 2019 by The Society for the New Message

All rights reserved. No part of this publication may be reproduced, stored in a retrieval system or transmitted in any form or by any means, electronic, mechanical, photo-copying, recording or otherwise without the prior written permission of the publisher.

Edited by Darlene Mitchell
Cover and interior: Designed by Reed Summers

ISBN: 978-1-942293-44-6 (POD)
ISBN: 978-1-942293-45-3 (ebook)
NKL POD Version 7.06
Library of Congress Control Number: 2019936256

Publisher's Cataloging-in-Publication Data
(Prepared by The Donohue Group, Inc.)

Names: Summers, Marshall Vian, author.
Title: The power of knowledge : the greater intelligence within you / as
    revealed to Marshall Vian Summers.
Description: Boulder, CO : New Knowledge Library, the publishing imprint
    of The Society for the New Message, [2019] | "A book of the New Message
    from God."
Identifiers: ISBN 9781942293446 (POD) | ISBN 9781942293453 (ebook)
Subjects: LCSH: Society for the New Message--Doctrines. | Knowledge,
    Theory of (Religion) | Intellect--Religious aspects. | Spiritual Life.
    | Mystical union.
Classification: LCC BP605.S58 S862 2019 (print) | LCC BP605.S58 (ebook)
    | DDC 299/.93--dc23

The Power of Knowledge is a book of the New Message from God and is published by New Knowledge Library, the publishing imprint of The Society for the New Message. The Society is a religious non-profit organization dedicated to presenting and teaching a New Message for humanity. The books of New Knowledge Library can be ordered at www.newknowledgelibrary.org, your local bookstore and at many other online retailers.

The New Message is being studied in more than 30 languages in over 90 countries. *The Power of Knowledge* is being translated into the many languages of our world by a dedicated group of volunteer student translators from around the world. These translations will all be available online at www.newmessage.org.

The Society for the New Message
P.O. Box 1724   Boulder, CO 80306-1724
(303) 938-8401   (800) 938-3891
011 303 938 84 01 (International)   (303) 938-1214 (fax)
newmessage.org   newknowledgelibrary.org
email: society@newmessage.org

We shall speak of God, the Higher Authority.

———————

The Higher Authority is speaking to you now, speaking through the Angelic Presence, speaking to a part of you that is the very center and source of your Being.

———————

The Higher Authority has a Message for the world, and for each person in the world.

———————

The Higher Authority is calling to you, calling to you down through the Ancient Corridors of your mind, calling to you beyond your beliefs and your preoccupations.

———————

For God has spoken again and the Word and the Sound are in the world.

From *God Has Spoken Again,*
Chapter 3: The Engagement

THE
POWER
OF
KNOWLEDGE

TABLE OF CONTENTS

Introduction i

CHAPTER 1   The Greater Power within You 1

CHAPTER 2   The Power of Knowledge 5

CHAPTER 3   The Soul's Journey on Earth 23

CHAPTER 4   Living in Separation 39

CHAPTER 5   The Crisis 55

CHAPTER 6   The Presence 67

CHAPTER 7   The Reconciliation 83

CHAPTER 8   Who You Are Is Not Your Mind 95

CHAPTER 9   Knowledge and the Limits of Belief 105

CHAPTER 10   The Greater Intelligence 123

CHAPTER 11   The Bridge 137

CHAPTER 12   Following the Presence 147

CHAPTER 13   The Spiritual Fire 165

CHAPTER 14   The Remembrance 175

Important Terms 185

The Story of the Messenger 193

The Voice of Revelation 195

About The Society for the New Message from God 197

About the Worldwide Community of the New Message from God 199

INTRODUCTION

The Power of Knowledge is a book of Revelation given by the Creator of all life to the human family through the Messenger Marshall Vian Summers.

Throughout history, God has given Revelation and Wisdom to meet the growing needs of our world at great turning points in the evolution of humanity. Now God is speaking again, delivering a New Revelation to meet the critical needs of humanity as it faces Great Waves of environmental, political and economic change and contact with a Greater Community of intelligent life in the universe.

God's progressive Revelation is continuing anew through a New Message from God, of which *The Power of Knowledge* is but a part. The words of this text are a direct communication from the Creator of all life, translated into human language by the Angelic Presence that watches over this world, and then spoken through the Messenger Marshall Vian Summers, who has given over 30 years of his life to this process of Revelation.

The New Message from God is an original communication from God to the heart of every person on Earth. It is not for one nation, one tribe or one religion alone. It is a Message for the entire world, a world facing very different needs and challenges from those of ancient times.

This communication is here to ignite the spiritual power of humanity, to sound God's calling for unity amongst the world's nations and religions, and to prepare humanity for a radically changing world and for its destiny in a larger universe of intelligent life.

The New Message from God speaks on nearly every aspect of life facing people today. It is the largest Revelation ever given to humanity, given now to a literate world of global communication and growing global awareness. Never before has there been a

i

THE POWER OF KNOWLEDGE

Divine Revelation of this size, given by God to all people of the world at once, in the lifetime of the Messenger.

Yet the New Message from God has not entered the world through the existing religious authorities and institutions of today. It has not come to the leaders of religion or to those who garner fame and recognition. Instead, it has been given to a humble man chosen and sent into the world for this one task, to be a Messenger for this New Message for humanity.

The Messenger has walked a long and difficult road to bring the New Message from God to you and to the world. The process of Revelation began in 1982 and continues to this day. The Messenger's story is one of perseverance, humility and lifelong service to others. His presence in the world today represents an opportunity to know him and receive the Revelation directly from him.

At the center of the New Message is the original Voice of Revelation, which has spoken the words of every book of the New Message. Never before has the Voice of Revelation, the Voice that spoke to the Messengers and prophets of the past, been recorded in its original purity and made available to each person to hear and to experience for themselves. In this way, the Word and the Sound of God's Revelation are in the world.

In this remarkable process of spoken Revelation, the Presence of God communicates beyond words to the Angelic Assembly that oversees the world. The Assembly then translates this communication into human language and speaks all as one through their Messenger, whose voice becomes the vehicle for this greater Voice—the Voice of Revelation.

The words of this Voice have been recorded in audio form, transcribed and are now available in the books of the New Message. In addition, the original audio recordings of the Voice of Revelation are available for all to hear. In this way, the purity of God's original spoken Message is preserved and given to all people in the world.

INTRODUCTION

At this time, the Messenger is engaged in compiling over three decades of spoken Revelation into a final and complete text—The One Book of the New Message from God. This book of Revelation will ultimately be divided into six volumes and possibly more. Each volume will contain two or more books, and each book will be organized by chapter and verse. Therefore, the New Message from God will be structured in the following way: Volume > Book > Chapter > Verse.

The Power of Knowledge is the fifth book of Volume 1 of the New Message from God and *The Power of Knowledge* contains 14 individual revelations (chapters) revealed to the Messenger at different times. The Messenger has compiled these revelations into the text you see today.

In order to bring this spoken communication into written form, slight textual and grammatical adjustments were made by the Messenger. This was requested of him by the Angelic Assembly to aid the understanding of the reader and to convey the Message according to the grammatical standards of the written English language.

In some instances, the Messenger has inserted a word not originally spoken in the Revelation. When present, you will often find this inserted word in brackets. Consider these bracketed words as direct clarifications by the Messenger, placed in the text by him alone in order to ensure that ambiguities in the spoken communication do not cause confusion or incorrect interpretations of the text.

In some cases, the Messenger has removed a word to aid the readability of the text. This was usually done in the case of certain conjunctions (words such as *and, but*) that made the text unnecessarily awkward or grammatically incorrect.

The Messenger alone has made these slight changes and only to convey the original spoken communication with the greatest clarity

THE POWER OF KNOWLEDGE

possible. None of the original meaning or intention of the communication has been altered.

The text of this book has been structured by the Messenger into verse. Each verse roughly signals the beginning or ending of a distinct message point communicated by the Source.

The verse structure of the text allows the reader to access the richness of the content and those subtle messages that may otherwise be missed in longer paragraphs of text that convey multiple topics. In this way, each topic and idea communicated by the Source is given its own standing, allowing it to speak from the page directly to the reader. The Messenger has determined that structuring the text in verse is the most efficacious and faithful way of rendering the original spoken revelations of the New Message.

Through this text, we are witnessing the process of preparation and compilation being undertaken by the Messenger, in his own time, by his own hands. This stands in stark contrast to the fact that the former great traditions were rarely put into written form by their Messengers, leaving the original messages vulnerable to alteration and corruption over time.

Here the Messenger seals in purity the texts of God's New Message and gives them to you, to the world and to all people in the future. Whether this book is opened today or 500 years from now, God's original communication will speak from these pages with the same intimacy, purity and power as it did the day it was first spoken.

Though it appears to be a book in the hand, *The Power of Knowledge* is something far greater. It is a calling and a communication from the Heart of God to you. In the pages of this book, God's Presence calls to you and to all people, calling for you to awaken from the dream and nightmare of living in Separation apart from your Source, calling to the presence of "Knowledge," the deeper spiritual Intelligence that lives within you, waiting to be discovered.

INTRODUCTION

The Power of Knowledge is part of a living communication from God to humanity. Remarkably, you have found the New Message from God, or it has found you. It is no coincidence that this is the case. This opens the next chapter in the mystery of your life and of your presence in the world at this time. The door opens before you. You need only enter to begin.

As you enter more deeply into the Revelation, the impact on your life will grow, bringing a greater experience of clarity, inner certainty and true direction to your life. In time, your questions will be answered as you find growing freedom from self-doubt, inner conflict and the restraints of the past. Here the Creator of all life is speaking to you directly, revealing to you the greater life that you were always destined to live.

The Society for the New Message from God

CHAPTER 1

THE GREATER POWER
WITHIN YOU

As revealed to
Marshall Vian Summers
on September 12, 2008
in Boulder, Colorado

People everywhere are carrying a greater power within themselves, a
power that they have not yet discovered. It is a deeper Intelligence
that the Creator of all life has given to each person.

This deeper Intelligence does not function like your intellect. It is
not conditioned by the world. It is not subject to doubt and fear,
confusion, resentment or anger. It is quiet. It is clear. It is powerful.
It cannot be persuaded by any force or power, for it only answers
to God.

This greater Intelligence is called Knowledge, and it lives within you,
beneath the surface of your mind. Every day Knowledge is giving you
counsel—to protect you, to guide you, to lead you. But if you are
living at the surface of your mind, caught up in the turbulence of the
surface, like the turbulence at the surface of the ocean, you will not
hear these messages. You will not feel this greater presence within
yourself. You will not recognize Knowledge's warnings and direction.

People try to keep themselves constantly stimulated—radio and
television, books and endless conversation, keeping themselves at
the surface of their mind, where they cannot feel the presence of

1

THE POWER OF KNOWLEDGE

Knowledge or the power of Knowledge, where they cannot hear or respond to the guidance that Knowledge is providing for them.

Perhaps once in a while they will feel a deeper inclination. They will recognize a sign or have a profound feeling about something, but these experiences are often intermittent and are often misinterpreted. Even people who feel that they are intuitive by nature often misinterpret the signs that they are receiving, trying to have everything fit in with what they want, to fulfill their desires and their goals, or to support a philosophy they have about life. So while many people do respond to the power and the presence of Knowledge, often they misinterpret its signs, thinking it is something else.

Some people think that every sign from within themselves must be about love, when in fact Knowledge is warning you about things. It is alerting you to the presence of danger. It is trying to restrain you from making critical mistakes, or from giving your life away to people or things that have no real value or future.

This is love also—the guidance of love, the restraint of love, the warnings from love. Yet if you think love is all about happiness and peace and pleasantness, then you do not understand the real power and potency of love. The love that a parent has for their child, the concern a parent will have for their child and the parents' attempt to protect their child from harm, danger or damaging influences represent the kind of love that lives within you.

How can you experience this Knowledge, which holds for you your greater purpose for coming into the world and can teach you to navigate the difficult times ahead under any kind of circumstances? How can you experience this for yourself?

THE GREATER POWER WITHIN YOU

You must learn to become still. You must learn to listen deep within yourself, not just for moments here or there, but on a more regular basis, as part of your spiritual practice. When you come to pray, do not simply ask for things, but learn to listen. God has already placed the answer within you, but it is deep within you, and you must go beneath the surface of your mind to experience it.

Like the ocean, the surface is turbulent and erratic, always changing, but deep down inside, deep within the ocean, there are strong currents that are moving the waters of the world. Your mind is like this. At the surface, it is swept up by the dangers and concerns of your outer life. It is persuaded and influenced and impacted by the world around you—by the opinions of other people, by the requirements of your life, by your desires and by your fears. But deep down there is a deeper current of life that is not subject to these outer influences. It is strong. It is permanent. It has a true direction. It is moving your life.

As you learn to take the Steps to Knowledge, you will learn to feel the presence of this greater Intelligence. And over time, you will learn to correctly discern its signs and its messages, and to accept its presence and its power in your life.

This is how God will speak to you. This is how God will influence you to protect you and to guide you towards leading and experiencing a greater life in the world—a life in service to the world, a life that is connected to the real world around you. This is the greatest discovery in life, and it is awaiting you.

Already, you have experienced the power and the presence of Knowledge at moments in your life when you felt an overwhelming desire to take a certain kind of action, or a concern about an event

THE POWER OF KNOWLEDGE

before it happened, or a concern about a loved one, only to find that that concern was well justified.

There is a power within you that is wise. It is moving you forward in some ways and holding you back in others. It represents your deeper conscience, the conscience that God has placed within you. You may ask God for miracles. You may ask God to intervene in your life. But God has put the answer in you already: the power and the presence of Knowledge, the deeper eternal Mind within you. It alone knows who you are and why you are here, who you must meet in this life and what you are here ultimately to contribute in service to humanity and to the world.

You carry the great endowment within yourself. It is waiting to be discovered. It is waiting for you to take the Steps to Knowledge, and to build the wisdom that you will need to have to carry this Knowledge out into the world, to protect this Knowledge and to discern its guidance and to experience its gifts.

This is the blessing that the Creator of all life has given to you and to each person. And the extent to which Knowledge can be experienced and expressed in this world, the world will be blessed, great disasters will be prevented, and humanity will continue to move in a positive direction.

This is the antidote to evil. This is the blessing for the world, a blessing that lives within you.

CHAPTER 2

THE POWER OF KNOWLEDGE

As revealed to
Marshall Vian Summers
on March 26, 2008
in Boulder, Colorado

God has given every person a deeper Intelligence, an Intelligence that is not affected by the world, that is not a product of social conditioning, an Intelligence that is not influenced by the powerful social influence that exists within your family and culture.

This deeper Intelligence within you is here to guide you, to protect you and to enable you to discover and to fulfill the greater purpose that has sent you into the world. This deeper Intelligence does not think and deliberate like your personal mind, like your surface mind, like the mind that has been conditioned by your family and your culture and your religions.

This is the Mind of God within you, a greater Intelligence that only responds to God and that is completely neutral and compassionate regarding the world. It is here to provide assurance that you will be able to find and fulfill your greater purpose, the greater purpose for which you have come here, to serve the world in its present condition and to lay the foundation for humanity's future, a future that will be unlike the past.

This greater Intelligence, this spiritual Intelligence that lives within you, exists beyond your intellect. It exists beyond your speculation. It exists beyond your understanding.

THE POWER OF KNOWLEDGE

Your work now is not to try to comprehend or to try to control this greater Intelligence within you, but to learn to respond to it, to recognize its signs and to follow its guidance. Your responsibility is to discern this greater Intelligence within you, to follow its signs, to heed its warnings and to follow its guidance as it prepares a greater life for you, as it frees you from the past, as it frees you from your own predicaments, as it takes you into new territory and creates greater opportunities for you.

Before this greater Intelligence can be discovered, people live according to their ideas and their beliefs, and the ideas and beliefs and expectations of others. They live at the very surface of their mind, governed by their social conditioning, governed by their fears and preferences and governed by the prevailing beliefs and attitudes of their culture. Whether they are conformists or rebels, they will follow this culture. It will determine their thinking, their feelings, their decisions and their perception of the world.

But there is a greater Intelligence within you that is not influenced by these things. It is called Knowledge. It is called Knowledge because it is related to your ability to know things directly. This experience of knowing things directly is not the product of rational thinking; it is not the result of accumulation of evidence; it is not the product of speculation, argument or debate.

So fundamental this is to your well-being and to your understanding of yourself. For intellectually you cannot understand yourself, really. You can catalogue your ideas and beliefs, your predispositions, your fears, your patterns of thought and so forth, but this does not really tell you who you are. This only chronicles the degree to which you have been conditioned by the world and your own human frailties.

6

THE POWER OF KNOWLEDGE

You have a relationship with God fundamentally, and this relationship is connected through Knowledge, and it is expressed through Knowledge.

This is not merely a matter of faith. Faith is what you exercise when you are not experiencing Knowledge—faith in Knowledge, faith in God, faith in something greater within yourself and within other people. But faith is only relevant to your personal mind, to your surface mind. To Knowledge itself, it is not an issue, for there is no doubt in Knowledge. It is not a mind that is full of doubt and fear and apprehension.

For Knowledge within you is not afraid of the world. It is not afraid of loss and deprivation. It is not afraid of death, for it cannot die, you see. Therefore, it has immense confidence and tremendous certainty. Because it cannot be influenced or corrupted by the world, it is the one thing within you that is really reliable.

Your thoughts are not reliable; they are changing all the time. Your beliefs are not reliable because they are merely a collective set of agreements between people. If they are based upon false assumptions, then everyone is agreeing upon something that is inherently untrue and inaccurate.

You have faith in God when you are not experiencing God, when you are not experiencing Knowledge. For Knowledge is how you experience God, you see. You may try to have fantastic visions, elevated experiences, moments of impassioned exuberance, but that is not really your relationship with God. For relationships are based upon what you can do together, how you are united both in essence and in action. For you live in a world of action, so to experience the

7

THE POWER OF KNOWLEDGE

Essence of God is not enough to fulfill your relationship here. It must be a relationship in action as well as a relationship in essence.

What does this mean, a relationship in action? It means you are here to do something together, in concert with one another. This is how Knowledge is really experienced. This is where its power and its efficacy begin to arise in your awareness and to manifest in your life. This is where your relationship with God really comes alive and becomes a foundation within yourself and a reference point for all your decisions.

To the intellect, Knowledge seems like a phantom, like a remote possibility, like something that is here to serve the mind. So the mind prays for what it wants because it is afraid. It prays for what it needs because it is lacking. It believes that if there is such a thing as Knowledge, it is here to serve the mind, to give the mind what it wants or needs and to fulfill what the mind believes already. In fact, people assume that God is here to serve their mind, to validate their ideas, to fulfill their expectations, to satisfy their desires.

But, you see, this is all backwards. It is fundamentally incorrect. Its ignorance and its arrogance become quite apparent when you really consider it. But people live within their surface mind, and so they think everything revolves around that. The whole universe revolves around their ideas about themselves.

For what is the mind at the surface but a vast collection of ideas and assumptions? There is really no essence here at all. There is nothing permanent here at all, and that is why people become so fixed upon their beliefs, so adamant about their ideas, and why they seek agreement from others so that their ideas can seem to become reality itself.

THE POWER OF KNOWLEDGE

People proclaim their certainty about God and God's Work and God's Word and God's Message and God's Messengers. This is an example of people trying to believe that God serves their ideas. So fixated they are upon their beliefs and assumptions, they cannot imagine that anything exists beyond them that is real and fundamental and inherently true.

However, this is the case, you see. Your ideas are only ideas. There is a far greater truth and reality beyond them. But ideas are important because they either let you see this Greater Reality, or they prevent you from seeing it altogether.

So the quality of one's ideas are important, and that is why, in the study of Steps to Knowledge, the New Message Book of Practices, you learn how to think the way that Knowledge thinks. You learn how to think constructively. You learn how to use the mind, your personal surface mind, effectively so that it can work in harmony with the greater Intelligence within you rather than competing with it for power and for dominance.

Knowledge within you cannot arise if you are governed by your thoughts completely. If you think your ideas and your beliefs are reality itself, there will be no room for Knowledge to emerge, and you will be afraid of it—afraid it will threaten your ideas, afraid it will upset your goals and plans, afraid it will throw you into doubt and confusion regarding what you think is real, true and valuable.

Here you create a hostile environment within yourself for the truth to arise. Though you may believe in God, though you may worship God, there is nowhere in your experience for God's Wisdom to emerge. There is no room for God to guide you. You have set such strict limits on what God can be and what God can say and what

THE POWER OF KNOWLEDGE

God can do and what you can be and what you can say and what you can do, there is little or no room for God's Wisdom and Guidance to emerge within you.

Here you must recognize that your ideas and your beliefs are temporary experiences. There is nothing absolute about them. They are either helping you to see, to know and to act effectively, or they are hindering you. They are either allowing you to engage with Knowledge within yourself, or they are hindering or preventing this engagement.

Your ideas are meant to serve a Greater Reality, you see—not to compete with it, not to deny it, not to try to control it or determine its ultimate reality. Here Knowledge gives you certainty and power, but it also requires humility on your part.

The assertion of your ideas and beliefs here has to be tempered. For in essence you do not know who you are; you do not know why you are here; you do not even know what you are doing, really. You are going through the motions of fulfilling your obligations and trying to satisfy your ideas and your beliefs and your desires, but you really do not know what you are doing. You are just going through the motions because you are doing what you think you are supposed to be doing.

But underneath this is a tremendous well of uncertainty and anxiety, self-doubt, self-recrimination, judgment of others and tremendous fear of the world and the future, tremendous fear of change, tremendous fear of loss, deprivation and self-destruction.

People around you seem to be very certain, and they assert themselves perhaps, but underneath this is a tremendous well of fear,

THE POWER OF KNOWLEDGE

for they do not know what they are doing, really. They only think they know what they are doing, and so they are relying upon their thoughts and their beliefs to give them a sense of reality, purpose and direction. So if anything comes along to threaten those ideas, people act like their whole lives are being threatened, their whole lives are being challenged—so afraid they are of being wrong, of being invalidated.

The stronger amongst you can be the most foolish here. Those who claim to have certainty and power and who assert themselves and who admonish others with such certainty and self-righteousness, they are the weakest amongst you. Their foolishness now has taken on destructive manifestations. Their ignorance is hidden to them. They do not know how foolish they really are.

This is why often Knowledge emerges in times of great self-doubt, in the face of difficult and confounding decisions. This is why Knowledge will come to you when you feel like a failure, when you have made mistakes, because for these moments especially, you are allowing room within yourself for a greater Intelligence to emerge. God can speak to you now because you are more open to listening, because you recognize your needs, because you are more humble and receptive.

The problem here, you see, is not that Knowledge is difficult to find. The question is: "Do you really want it?" Or do you only want it to reassure you in times of doubt or to reinforce you in times of weakness? But the rest of the time, you want to be the captain of your ship. You do not really want to have a greater power emerge within yourself.

THE POWER OF KNOWLEDGE

This strikes at the very heart of Separation, you see, which is fundamentally a competition for power. You only want God to have power in your life when you yourself are feeling weak and helpless. But the rest of the time you want to have that power. It is a competition for power.

This is what created the Separation in the beginning and what maintains it, not only within you and throughout the world, but throughout the universe—that part of Creation where the separated live, which is a very small part of Creation, I can assure you, but certainly great enough to transcend your understanding and comprehension.

God has given you a perfect guiding Intelligence. It is not bound to give you what you want, but it is here to give you what you need. It is here to fulfill the greater need of your soul. It is not a slave to the mind. It is the master. Your mind must become the servant.

Here the true hierarchy of authority can become established, where your body serves your mind, your mind serves Knowledge and Knowledge serves God. This is the great peacemaker in the world, for Knowledge within you cannot be in conflict with Knowledge within others. You may have a different interpretation. Knowledge may assert itself differently and uniquely within you, and it will to some degree, but fundamentally you cannot be at war with another if you are both guided by Knowledge.

For Knowledge cannot attack itself, and that is why Knowledge is the great need of the world. It is the great need of the individual. It is the great need between nations and groups. The degree to which it has been realized and expressed will determine whether a nation will go

THE POWER OF KNOWLEDGE

to war or will continue to try to build a foundation for peace and peaceful relations.

You look out into the world and you see there is so little evidence of Knowledge in people's thinking and behavior. People are governed by fear. They are governed by the fear of loss and deprivation. They are governed by their own desires. They are governed by their grievances and their distrust. And it is shocking that you live in a world without Knowledge.

Yet Knowledge is here. It is within each person, waiting to be discovered. Your great task in life—beyond mere survival, beyond the fulfillment of your basic needs—is to find and to follow Knowledge, to take the Steps to Knowledge.

Without this, you are operating on assumptions only. You are going into the future blind, governed by past conditioning that cannot account for events that are occurring now, that cannot anticipate the future, that cannot see the signs of the world. You are going into the future blind. You are living blind—governed by thoughts that are not even your own, governed by attitudes and beliefs that you have adopted from your culture, from your family and your society. You do not even know what you think as an individual. And the great problems you see emerging in the world around you and the confounding problems you see even within yourself—your own internal conflicts, your own difficulties and disposition—you cannot even understand how these can be resolved.

But no matter how confounding the problems of the world, no matter how confounding the issues and problems you may see within yourself, God has provided an answer, and the answer is the greater Intelligence that is here to move your life in a new direction.

THE POWER OF KNOWLEDGE

You cannot use Knowledge to enrich yourself, to get what you want, to overcome others, but you can follow Knowledge to learn how to build a new foundation in your life.

Allow Knowledge to show you what is important and to restore to you your self-confidence and your ability to understand others, your ability to experience and to express love, and the greater wisdom that Knowledge will provide for you in learning how to navigate a difficult and changing world. No matter how confounding the problems may seem to be and your inability to understand or to resolve them, there is Knowledge within you.

You see, Knowledge is not here simply to solve problems. It is here to give you a greater life, to take you into service to the world in the way that is most meaningful and important for you. It is meant to engage you with certain people at a much higher level, at the level of higher purpose. The direction it sets for you in your life is set to enable you to discover these things, and to establish a new kind of relationship with yourself and with others and with the world itself.

Here your role will not be grandiose. You will not be a savior or an avatar, but your service will be very important and will help to initiate Knowledge in others. For Knowledge ultimately is your greatest gift. The demonstration of Knowledge—the reality of Knowledge—is the greatest gift. You can feed people, and this will be increasingly necessary in the difficult times to come. You can help people in many, many ways. That is very important and authentic. But your greatest gift will be Knowledge. For here you are giving them a reminder that they have a connection with God, and you are demonstrating this connection yourself through your thinking and your behavior.

THE POWER OF KNOWLEDGE

If you want God to help you, you must build a relationship with Knowledge, for this is how God will speak to you. This is how God will move you, and guide you, and restrain you, and hold you back, and lead you forward. If you want the Power of God to be of service in your life and to others through you, then you must bring your power in service to God's Power and not compete, and not deny, and not struggle.

Ultimately, this gives you peace and resolution because the war within you will be over—the war between what you want and what you know, between the desires of the mind and the certainty of Knowledge within you, the war between yourself and God that created the Separation.

For God is not at war with you, certainly, but you are still at war with God because you want to be god. You want to be the god of your life. You want to create your own reality. You want to live apart from God. And this motivation is still there, you see. It is important to face this and not deny it. It is creating the world that you see. It is motivating human behavior everywhere.

You have a greater destiny in the world. God has sent you here to accomplish specific tasks with specific people. The knowledge of this is kept within your Knowledge. The guidance to accomplish this is within your Knowledge. The meaning of this contribution to the world is kept safely within your Knowledge.

You cannot figure it out. You cannot understand it with the intellect. You can only follow it and serve it and use the powers of the intellect to help you do this.

THE POWER OF KNOWLEDGE

Fundamentally, its reality is beyond your comprehension, but that is fine. Life itself is beyond your comprehension. God is beyond your comprehension. Love is beyond your comprehension. Inspiration is beyond your comprehension. Yet you are meant to have and to experience all these things. You can be happy without knowing why. You can be joyful without self-evaluation. You can feel inspiration in your life without having a logical explanation for it.

Your great task now is to realize the need for Knowledge in your life—to have the honesty, the clarity and the humility to recognize that you are living a life that is disassociated from your greater purpose, that you are not fully connected with the real thread of truth in your life, that you are living out your ideas and beliefs and assumptions, fulfilling the expectations of others, going through the motions of life. But you are not yet fully alive. You are not really connected inside yourself to the deeper current of your life.

Recognize this. Accept this. And it opens the door, you see. It allows something greater to emerge, which will emerge slowly within you. You cannot have it all in the next ten minutes. You cannot have it all today. It will emerge slowly and give you time to recognize it, to adjust to it; time to reconsider your thoughts, your beliefs; time to re-evaluate your relationship with others, with your mind, with your body; time to go through a great transition from being an individual who is a product of social conditioning to becoming a man or woman of Knowledge, guided by a greater power now that is mysterious, yet whose presence and whose guidance produce the most practical and meaningful results.

This is your greater work, for your greater purpose in the world will be based upon your foundation in Knowledge, for it can only be known. It cannot be figured out through debate or speculation. It

THE POWER OF KNOWLEDGE

cannot be realized through intellectual effort without this greater power within you. For this is the power that holds your greater purpose and will give you the strength and the clarity to discover it, to experience it and to express it effectively in the world where it must be expressed. The way here is simple if you are not governed by your preferences.

God is close at hand, and God's Power that God has put within you to guide you, to protect you and to lead you to your great accomplishments is very close at hand. But you must create a place within yourself for them to emerge.

You must learn to ask questions without giving yourself the answers. You must learn to realize your deeper needs and the limits of your own ideas. And you must see the great need for Knowledge in the world around you as people desperately try to fulfill their fantasies and their desires, all the while disassociated from themselves and from the greater movement of life within them and around them. Instead of condemning the world, you must recognize the great need for Knowledge—within yourself, within others, within the entire human family.

You cannot live a greater life without Knowledge. You cannot know yourself without Knowledge. You will not be able to recognize and participate with those people who hold the greatest promise for you without Knowledge. You will not be able to realize that you live a greater life and that you have a greater destiny beyond the world without Knowledge. Even if you believe these things, you will not know them to be true. To be free from the constant aggravation of fear and anxiety, you must build your foundation in Knowledge, allow Knowledge to be the great presence within you, the ground of your Being, your fundamental reference point.

17

THE POWER OF KNOWLEDGE

Ask yourself, when you want something or desire something, ask Knowledge within you if it is important for you, and just see if there is a response. Your mind wants something, oh yes, it does. It wants this person; it wants to live in this place; it wants to have this wealth; it wants to have this privilege. But go to Knowledge within yourself and say, "Do you want these things for me?" And deep within you, you can feel the response.

In many cases, Knowledge will not respond because it is not important. It does not have this desire. And that right away tells you that you are going against yourself in wanting this person, this place, or this thing, whatever it may be. For your heart does not really want it. Your mind wants it. Your mind wants it because it is afraid, because it is insecure, because it is agitated, because it is uncomfortable, because it is without Knowledge to guide it. It is nervous always, restless, agitated, wanting this, wanting that, afraid of this, afraid of that. Never a moment of peace does it have.

So you go to Knowledge, and you say, "Well, is this important for me?" and you see that there is no response. In some cases, Knowledge will indicate adamantly, "No!" because in that case, you are wanting something that would really be harmful for you or that would take your life in the wrong direction, that would really set you back. In this case, Knowledge will create a sense of resistance and restraint within yourself. How many people have walked down the aisle on their marriage day feeling this great response and restraint as they were about to give their lives away to something that had no real promise or destiny?

Every bad decision you make, you will feel this resistance. You must learn to honor it. It is a sign. It means you must go to Knowledge. It means you must have a strong enough sense of the presence of

18

THE POWER OF KNOWLEDGE

Knowledge within yourself, a pervasive presence that is the ground of your Being—beneath and above and beyond your intellect.

People call this a "gut feeling" because it is experienced much more physically. But Knowledge is more than a gut feeling. It is a greater Intelligence within you. If it does not want something you think you want, then you should not pursue that thing. If it creates a sense of restraint or resistance, you must hold yourself back, for you are about to make a very dangerous and consequential decision.

In other things, Knowledge will give you the go ahead. It is an absolute "Yes! Do this. Be with this person. Go to this place. Take this action." You get a big green light within yourself because you have checked it out with yourself.

But, you see, people rarely ever do this. They simply go for what looks good. And every disaster that they create in their life always began with something looking good. They are lured by appearances—the promise of wealth, the promise of pleasure, the promise of love, the promise of happiness. They are lured by appearances.

If they went to Knowledge, they would see that the attraction was not real; that it was a deception, an illusion, a fantasy. They would see that if Knowledge is not swayed, they should not be swayed. If Knowledge is not impressed, they should not be impressed. If Knowledge is not taking the bait, they should not take the bait. This is the power of Knowledge within you. If Knowledge is at peace, they can be at peace. If Knowledge is not going anywhere, they do not need to go anywhere.

The more this becomes your experience, and it gradually will become your experience, the greater the certainty, the greater the confidence,

THE POWER OF KNOWLEDGE

the greater the equanimity you will experience in your life. For these things all come from Knowledge.

The New Message has provided the Steps to Knowledge. There are other teachings that provide steps to Knowledge, too. You must find the pathway that is correct for you. But once you find this pathway, you must go the whole way. Do not dabble with it. You will reach a point where you will want to quit, where you will be too uncertain to go on, where your mind will be swayed by other things, by other attractions. You will be distracted. But you must stay with your practice.

When you begin the Steps to Knowledge, you must continue. Go the whole way. Do not stop. It is like climbing a mountain, you see. You go a little ways and you think, "Oh, this is hard. This is steep. Do I really want to climb this mountain?" You doubt and you reconsider because it is not as easy as you thought it would be. But you must continue.

The power and the presence of Knowledge lives within you, waiting to be discovered. This is the real meaning of your spirituality. This is your spiritual work. If you are to have any hope of discovering your greater purpose in the world and of finding those greater relationships that are part of this purpose and can express this purpose, then you must take the Steps to Knowledge.

For within you, you have Knowledge, and you have your ideas. They should not be in competition with one another. Your mind is meant to serve Spirit, which is Knowledge. Knowledge is here to serve God and to fulfill your purpose for coming into the world and the greater need of your soul.

THE POWER OF KNOWLEDGE

Realize, then, the path has been made simple. It is not complex. The journey requires wisdom and re-evaluation, but it is not complex. The need of your soul is fundamental. It cannot be satisfied through the acquisition of people, places and things. It is here to fulfill something greater, and Knowledge within you knows what this is.

CHAPTER 3

THE SOUL'S JOURNEY ON EARTH

As revealed to
Marshall Vian Summers
on October 25, 2008
in Boulder, Colorado

You are traveling through time and space, engaged in a long
journey of return to your Ancient Home. In this life and beyond,
this journey continues. It is not a journey you make just for
yourself. It is a journey you make for all those who have lost
contact with the Creator of all life. It is a journey of Separation and
return. It is a journey towards a greater experience of your purpose
and your destiny.

The journey is so very different from what people imagine because
the imagination cannot contain a reality this great. Words, like ideas,
give limit and form to things, but they cannot encompass greater
realities. This requires reverence and resonance to experience the
truth at a larger level. Ideas and beliefs are fine for small things. But a
greater reality—the reality of your journey through time and space—
is beyond what your imagination or your intellect can conceive of at
this moment.

You can only give analogies here. But analogies cannot contain the
greater panorama of life of which you are a part nor the meaning of
your journey through this life and beyond. The heart can understand,
but the mind cannot contain a reality this big at the level of its own
ideas. That is why the reality is so very different from what so many
people think and believe.

THE POWER OF KNOWLEDGE

When the Separation from God began, you could not separate completely because a part of Creation is within you and has stayed within you, and you cannot get rid of it. It is as if God goes along for the ride. Wherever you go, God is there, within you and around you. You may say, "I don't want to believe in God. I don't want anything to do with religion." That is fine, but God is still within you, and God is all around you.

You may think, God is all about this teacher—my savior, my saint, my prophet—but God is still within you and all around you.

You may claim that God is responsible for events of the world or events of your life, but God is still within you and all around you.

The mind thinks, the mind admonishes others, the mind proclaims great truths according to its experience and range of understanding, but the reality is beyond this.

You are separated in your own mind, and the intellect is a product of this Separation. It thinks it is who you are. It thinks it knows what reality is. It thinks it is your soul and your Being. It thinks its thoughts represent its reality and distinguish it from other minds who have other thoughts. Your mind thinks that its reality is the reality of its ideas and its association with people, places and things. But who you really are is beyond all this.

Because God has remained within you, God's Knowledge has remained within you. And this Knowledge now is here to guide you, to protect you and to lead you into a greater experience of life so that the Separation within you may be dissolved. This purpose and this destiny that Knowledge holds for you is to contribute to a world in

THE SOUL'S JOURNEY ON EARTH

need, within the very circumstances that you see today and which will be arising in the future.

From the standpoint of Knowledge within you, you are here on a mission. You have a greater purpose for being here. You are not merely an animal trying to survive, trying to be satisfied, trying to be happy, trying to be secure. You are a Being from Heaven, who is part of the Separation, who is now here to work towards your own self-discovery and redemption.

While your mind continues to try to conceive of itself and attach itself to people, places and things, Knowledge within you is moving. It is advising you, it is counseling you. If you can hear it, you will benefit from it. But if you cannot hear it, then you cannot receive its wisdom, its blessing and its empowerment.

Your success in this life does not cast you to Heaven or to Hell, but sets you on the next stage of your journey. If you are to regain wisdom and compassion and a degree of self-awareness, then you will be prepared for a greater level of service.

People think this one life is their whole existence in physical reality. Some people even think that physical reality will come to a final ending point within their lifetime. These ideas are the result of the limits of your imagination. To conceive of your life continuing beyond this into other arenas of life and other levels of service is really too much for most people to consider. They do not have the capacity to think at this level.

So the idea of a Judgment Day is invented. But why would God judge you when God knows exactly why you are doing what you are doing and when God understands that the world is a place of such

THE POWER OF KNOWLEDGE

immense difficulty and persuasion that without Knowledge to guide an individual here, they would surely fall into error, sometimes grievous error?

God is not going to punish you for living in a state like this. God is going to call you to come to Knowledge within yourself, so that you may have the Power and the Presence of God to guide you, to protect you and to lead you forward.

There is no Judgment Day then. This is something people invent because they want justice to be carried out in Heaven where it is not carried out on Earth, according to their notions of what justice should be. They want the wicked to be punished, even if they themselves cannot punish those whom they think are in error. This is merely a projection.

The idea of an angry God has been promoted over time in many traditions to force allegiance of belief, to frighten people into believing in a particular religious idea or doctrine. People worship God, and their whole idea of God is based on a kind of subservient mentality where you have to please God or God will punish you. God will ruin your crops. God will bring pestilence. God will bring devastating weather. And so, over the course of time, people think they have to please God or they will face terrible consequences here on Earth.

But the truth is they have entered a reality that is by its very nature extremely difficult and problematic, a reality that is unpredictable and, though it follows basic patterns, is quite chaotic.

This is the physical universe that has been created as a place for the separated to live, in a separate reality. It is wonderful and terrible,

THE SOUL'S JOURNEY ON EARTH

beautiful and frightening. It is attractive and, in some cases, repulsive. It is so unlike your Ancient Home from which you have come and to which you will eventually return. And yet it is a place that requires contribution. It is a place of action. It is a place for giving. It is through this place that the soul must journey now.

You are in the world for a greater purpose. You did not invent this for yourself. You cannot change this purpose, but how and if it will be experienced is up to the events of time and to your own decisions regarding it. So while your purpose is pre-determined, the events of your life are not. At this level of existence, chance plays a very great role, and the importance of your decisions plays a very great role.

Some people want to think that God is controlling all of the events of life, but that is not true at all. God has set in motion the geological and biological forces that have shaped the evolution of life. But these forces are self-perpetuating and do not require God's intervention. So if the earthquake happens, it is part of the geological process. If famine and pestilence occur, it is largely the result of forces beyond your control.

God is not punishing you. But this is the reality where you must choose. It is whether you choose reunion with God or Separation from God. You choose this every day. You choose this in what you choose to think about, what you choose to believe in and how you choose to respond to difficulties and decisions in life.

Your mind is formed in isolation, and so it believes of itself as being a singular entity, an entity apart from other entities. It distinguishes itself and tries to use the body to distinguish itself. It is a product of Separation, and it reinforces Separation. But you also have a deeper Knowledge within you, a deeper Knowledge that has been placed

THE POWER OF KNOWLEDGE

there by God. It cannot be persuaded. It cannot be seduced. It cannot be induced to do things that go against its primary nature.

It is like you have two voices in your mind. You might have more than two voices, but they all come down to being a voice for Separation or a voice for reunion. But the voice for reunion does not think like your mind. It does not deliberate. It does not speculate. It does not judge and condemn. It does not base its reality on ideas or concepts or allegiances.

Your surface mind—your mind that has been shaped by culture, by your family, by tradition and by your response to a changing world—this mind must serve a greater Mind within you if it is to become redeemed and if its great abilities are to be utilized beneficially for your sake and for the sake of others.

That is why Knowledge has been placed within you to guide you. For God knows you would become lost in the world without this Knowledge. You would fall into error, and you would live a life of conflict, difficulty and self-repudiation.

Your journey, then, is to return to the power and presence of Knowledge. Or, said in other words, it is to become true to your deeper conscience, true to yourself, true to what you most deeply feel and know. This can be described within religious terms or outside of religious terms, but it amounts to the same thing.

With Knowledge, you discover you are here for a greater purpose, and you see that you are being guided in certain ways and restrained in other ways. As you gain more confidence, you are able to follow this and to receive its great blessings and its great lessons about life. You do this without condemnation of yourself or others. You do this

THE SOUL'S JOURNEY ON EARTH

in humility, realizing that you are following a greater power, a power that is beyond the scope and reach of the intellect. You place yourself here as a student, a student who presumes very little and is open to learn everything that must be learned.

Here you do not live according to answers, but you live with questions. The intellect cannot do this, for it is far too insecure. It must have answers, and so it provides its own answers. It is too insecure. It is too feeble to live with questions. That takes a greater strength within you. You live with questions you may never be able to answer, but you live with them because they open your mind, and they stimulate a deeper connection with Knowledge within yourself.

Knowledge is the answer because as you become stronger with Knowledge, you have greater certainty, you have greater confidence and you have greater strength and ability. You can face danger and uncertainty without anger and condemnation. You can face questions for which you do not have answers with inquiry, openness and humility. You have the power to restrain your self-destructive tendencies and to distinguish the thoughts in your mind that are truly beneficial from all of the thoughts that you have absorbed from the environment around you.

If you become strong with Knowledge in this life, you will be given a greater level of service beyond this world. This may be service in this world or in other worlds. It may be service as a transcendent teacher, one of the Unseen Ones who guides those who are still living in form. Or you may return to the manifest world as a great teacher, as someone who has great promise to shed wisdom and guidance and resolution in another existence.

THE POWER OF KNOWLEDGE

Here there is no Judgment Day. There is only progress. You cannot return to your heavenly state full of anger, resentment, self-judgment and condemnation of others. You cannot return to your heavenly state full of indecision and ambivalence, with addictions and self-destructive tendencies. You just simply cannot return in this state of mind.

To think that all these things can be resolved within one life is to underestimate the problem. Even if you could resolve all of these things in one life, your accomplishment would be so great that God would want to use you to help others who are still lost in their state of Separation. So you could not return to Heaven even under these circumstances.

God is going to get maximum use out of you and maximum use and benefit from whatever wisdom you can acquire living in the physical reality. This is not a punishment because what undoes all of the tendencies and the memories and the suffering born of Separation is contribution, is service. God does not merely dissolve all of these things within you because God did not create them. They must be dissolved within you, by you and through you, by taking a different course in life.

Your errors are replaced with service. The service comes from deep within you. It is not a scheme that you create to try to offset guilt within yourself. It is something that emanates from Knowledge within you. It replaces the memory of Separation with the memory of contribution, communication and connection with others. It is by following the true master within yourself that your previous errors in judgment and unhappy experiences are erased and forgotten.

THE SOUL'S JOURNEY ON EARTH

People cannot see this because they cannot imagine what Heaven is like. When you are living in the world, thinking you are an individual, you cannot imagine what Heaven is like. For imagination is how you give form to your ideas, and the form is extremely limited and temporary. That is why you cannot imagine permanent things. You cannot imagine peace. Everything you imagine is limited and temporary in nature.

Your experience of this happens at a deeper level. The mind can only imagine things it can think of. But if it cannot think of Creation except in very limited terms in time and space, then obviously you must experience your deeper nature beyond the realm of your intellect.

Your intellect is how you evaluate life from a position of Separation. But if the Separation is not real and can never be complete, then your ideas must be relative in nature. Perhaps you can see the truth of things in time, of momentary things. You can solve problems because that is what the intellect is for. It is to solve problems within a limited range of your experience in this life.

This is the real value of the intellect. In service to Knowledge, it is a wonderful instrument of communication. That is what it is for, and that is what redeems it and gives it a greater purpose and a greater meaning.

Your happiness in life will be born of your connection to Knowledge and the great service it will render through you, and the redemption it will give to your mind and to your emotions. You will finally begin to feel right within yourself and outgrow the discomforts that attended you before. It will free you from giving your life away to people and things and places inappropriately and prematurely. It will

THE POWER OF KNOWLEDGE

free you from all the suffering of indecision, self-doubt and self-recrimination. It will do this gradually because it takes time to change, to shift your allegiance within yourself—allegiance from your ideas and the ideas of others to a deeper power that is guiding you from within yourself. You begin to recognize this power in others and to see its central importance in your life and in the welfare of all of humanity.

You do not need to concern yourself with what is beyond the world because you have not reached that junction yet. Your mind cannot conceive of your life before this world except in historical terms and in imaginary terms. Perhaps you will have certain memories of things that happened before, and those could be real. But they are out of context, and you cannot understand them fully.

It is this life to which you must give your attention. You are here for a greater purpose. Only Knowledge within you knows what this purpose is and holds this purpose for you.

This is the journey that you are taking, and you are taking it step by step in stages. As Knowledge becomes realized within you and you are able to follow it in specific matters, your experience of it will grow stronger. And you will realize that redemption has been placed within you to guide you, and that redemption is not just a product of believing in concepts or accepting doctrines or going through the motions of expressing devotion to a supreme power in the universe. Really, your responsibility to God is to discover, to accept and to express this greater purpose that has brought you into the world. To do this, you must follow Knowledge, allowing Knowledge to be mysterious, for it exists beyond the realm of your intellect.

THE SOUL'S JOURNEY ON EARTH

This leads to a great re-evaluation of your life. For with Knowledge, you see things differently, and your values change, and your priorities change. Perhaps you have experienced some of this change already.

When you begin to experience Knowledge, you seek quiet instead of stimulation. You seek honest engagement with others instead of meaningless conversation. You seek the experience of union in relationships rather than just using another to gain personal advantage. You value your insights more than your thoughts. You begin to see over time that who you are is not your mind, and that your mind is really a wonderful instrument of communication for the Spirit, for Knowledge. You see your body as a vehicle for being in the world, a vehicle through which communication can flow, through which contribution can occur and through which a deeper association with others who are here in the world can be experienced.

You are here on a journey in the world. You have the choice of whether to be lost in the world or to be able to experience a greater purpose and reality being in the world. These two approaches render an entirely different experience of life from one another. You can look around you to see the consequences dramatically being portrayed by people choosing to live in Separation, and the suffering and the uncertainty and the disastrous decisions that result from taking and maintaining this position.

If you look, you will find there are far fewer examples of people following Knowledge. You will see the evidence of Knowledge in their lives, and this will inspire you and remind you that Knowledge lives within you as well and that wherever you go and whatever you do, God is there.

THE POWER OF KNOWLEDGE

You have a deeper conscience that tells you when you are doing something that is good and when you are doing something that is not good for you. In time, you will learn that when you see error in others, it is a demonstration that they are not being with Knowledge, and you will use this to reinforce your commitment to Knowledge. Rather than condemning the person or the situation, you will see the great need for Knowledge.

With Knowledge, there will be no war and conflict. People may disagree about how to do things, but they will resonate regarding what must be done, what must be resolved. Knowledge is united within people and between people. It is the great peacemaker in the world. It is the power that overrides the tendencies to condemn, to attack, to act selfishly and to seek to conquer others for your own benefit.

It is as if you have competing forces within yourself. They are entirely different. They have entirely different directions. They cast an entirely different experience and understanding of life. They are leading you in different directions.

So every day you choose which to follow, what to honor and what to look for in yourself and in others. As this becomes a conscious act, then you will feel you have a much greater authority and ability to determine the kind of experience you will have.

If you go with Knowledge, you will feel good, and you will resonate with yourself. If you go against Knowledge, you will be uncomfortable, as if a betrayal has occurred.

You can go against Knowledge for many different reasons: for wealth; to acquire beauty; to acquire people, places and things. But within

THE SOUL'S JOURNEY ON EARTH

yourself you will not feel good about it. If you choose anger and condemnation of others, you will feel very bad within yourself. You might feel justified, you might think that you are in the right, but you will feel bad within yourself. Your deeper conscience is being violated, and you will feel bad within yourself.

You may try to create your own reality and make your life into whatever you think it should be or that you want it to be, but you cannot violate your deeper conscience without creating suffering within yourself.

Here what is good and what is bad are merely known. In the complexities of trying to resolve problems and dilemmas, this basic conscience can be clouded, and it might be more difficult to recognize what is the correct way to go. Here the intellect comes into its real service. It must determine how things should be brought about. It deals with the details, dealing with specifics, but the real direction must be set by Knowledge.

You have an ethical and moral foundation within yourself that was created by God. Even if it conflicts with your cultural values and with your social conditioning, it cannot be changed. Your culture may teach you to condemn others and to punish others for certain behaviors, or to distrust other groups or other tribes or other nations. But this is a violation of your deeper conscience. So you have a social conscience that is your social conditioning, but then you have a deeper conscience that was created by God.

It is the great blessing of your life that the Separation never could be complete, and that within yourself what God has created remains. It is this that will save you. It is this that will guide you and restrain you from giving your life away and from making critical mistakes.

35

THE POWER OF KNOWLEDGE

The world is the perfect place to reunite with Knowledge, for the need is immense. Without Knowledge you are lost, with only your desires and your fears to guide you.

You do not have to be religious. You do not have to belong to a religious group or adhere to a religious teaching to return to the power and presence of Knowledge within yourself. It will serve you within or beyond a religious tradition in any world, in any nation, in any culture, in any situation.

But here so many people are strangers unto themselves. It is to be reacquainted and reunited with Knowledge that represents your most fundamental need in life. Beyond acquiring food and shelter and the basic necessities of survival, this is your most fundamental endeavor.

To take the Steps to Knowledge, to become a student of Knowledge, to learn The Way of Knowledge is to learn the way of a greater life. You need this every day, in every one of your decisions. You need this to escape from the Hell that you have created for yourself—from the Hell of uncertainty, from the Hell of self-judgment, from the Hell of insecurity, from the Hell of anxiety, from the Hell of fear and from the Hell of condemnation of yourself and others.

When you realize that this is Hell, and that it is not just your normal state, you will begin to look more deeply for the evidence of Knowledge. When you realize how much you are suffering, how much you are losing and how many mistakes you are making, you will want to find the source of certainty within yourself and within others. You will want this certainty to be the basis of your decision making and the foundation of any relationship that you establish with another person.

THE SOUL'S JOURNEY ON EARTH

God has sent you into the world to contribute unique gifts involving certain people in certain situations. You must find these people, and you must find these situations. You will feel an urgency here. Even if you misconstrue these deeper needs, they will exist within you. They will lead you on.

In the meantime, you marry people, you become attached to places, you give your life to certain things. But these deeper needs remain, and until they are met, you will be restless, you will feel that your life must move on, you will not be content with what you have. For these represent the deeper needs of the soul, the most fundamental needs within you.

The soul's needs can only be met by your discovering and fulfilling your greater purpose here. Since your intellect cannot figure this out, you must follow the guidance of Knowledge. And you must learn of the power and the presence of Knowledge within your life.

It is really very simple, but it will not seem simple because your mind will be confused. Because Knowledge is mysterious, it does not fit in with your ideas. You cannot control it; you cannot define it; you cannot express it to your friends in words because Knowledge is a profound experience of seeing, knowing and acting. It will seem rare and confusing at the outset, but in time you will see that it is the most natural thing for you to do.

This is your journey in the world. It is a journey that will continue beyond this world. It is a journey that you cannot define by ideas alone. Knowledge will take you on this journey, and it will give meaning, purpose and direction to your life.

THE POWER OF KNOWLEDGE

You will see that there is a deeper current of your life. Beyond all of your thoughts and the events of the day, there is a deeper current running in your life. This is what will give you strength and purpose and wisdom as you proceed.

It is necessary here for you to realize that who you are is not your mind, not your thoughts, not your beliefs and that your true existence is beyond them—beyond these things and that God is beyond these things. An idea cannot be a replacement for a real relationship. And real relationships transcend your ideas. Your real relationship with God transcends your ideas, or the ideas of your culture or your religion.

In time, you will shift your allegiance to the power of Knowledge. This is shifting your allegiance to God. This is undoing the Separation at the very foundation of your Being.

Here you are able to use the mind rather than being ruled by it. Here you are able to use thoughts and definitions instead of being ruled by them. Here you will be able to use the marvelous capabilities of your intellect and your body instead of being a slave to them.

This is a practical form of liberation, and it will return you to your most essential nature, and to the greater purpose that has brought you here, into the world, at this time.

CHAPTER 4

LIVING IN SEPARATION

As revealed to
Marshall Vian Summers
on March 3, 2011
in Boulder, Colorado

You are living in a state of Separation—as a singular person, seemingly distinct from all other singular persons, distinct from other life forms, with a singular identity and awareness.

You are with others, but essentially alone. You can create your own thoughts. You can imagine whatever you like based upon your experience in the world. If you have political freedom and social mobility, you can even set your own direction in life.

You seem to be alone in the privacy of your own mind and thoughts. You may even think that your thoughts are your thoughts, but the vast majority of them you have accumulated and absorbed from people and society around you.

You hope and pray that life will be good to you, but calamity is always possible, and things can change in a moment. Now the world is undergoing great and convulsive change, Great Waves of change, and there is a greater sense of uncertainty and anxiety about the future and what may be coming over the horizon.

To be alone is to be afraid—to be afraid of pain, to be afraid of loss, to be afraid of rejection, to be afraid of criticism, to be afraid you will not have what you need or what you want. And, of course, this

THE POWER OF KNOWLEDGE

becomes the source of aberrant behavior, dishonesty, manipulation, avoidance, distractions, indulgences, obsessions, addictions—everything.

The world you live in seems to be a world of the separated. Creatures in nature are competing with each other and devouring each other. People get along superficially in order to maintain social order, but it seems that real devotion, especially to one beyond your family, [is] rare and exceptional.

It is a hopeless situation. People have tried a thousand escapes and avoidances, but never can they seem to escape their fundamental dilemma—the dilemma of Separation.

Though the world has great beauty and nature is fascinating, it is difficult to be truly happy and at ease in the physical environment. It is demanding. It requires constant problem solving and adaptation. It is complex, particularly if you are engaged with many people. It is vexing. It is confusing. And it is hazardous.

Even nature itself, if you were to face it honestly, has many hazards. For though it seems that you care for nature, it does not seem to care for you. You care for nature and its beauty, and to maintain its diversity and its essential qualities, but nature does not seem to care whether you live or die. You are just a feature of the landscape, a temporary feature.

This, of course, is a stark picture, but it is an honest one. When you set aside your avoidances and your dishonesty, your preferences, your dreams and fantasies, you will have to come to this essential reckoning within yourself.

LIVING IN SEPARATION

It can be a hard landing for many people as they find themselves all of a sudden facing illness, financial deprivation, the prospect of loss and greater loss, problems in relationships, problems with health, problems with employment, problems even, for the poorer people, with survival itself.

Yet within this hopeless situation, with seemingly no real and substantive remedy, God has created the antidote, the antidote to Separation. For part of you has not separated from God. It never separated from God. It is connected to God already, completely.

This part of you exists beyond the realm and the reach of the intellect. For the intellect was mostly created as a sophisticated intelligence to navigate the difficulties of living in physical reality. It is a marvelous instrument, but it is not who you really are. You are not your mind. But if you are not your mind, then what are you? It seems a great void, a great mystery, a great question.

God has given an answer to the problem that seems to have no answer—a pathway out of Separation, a pathway that does not divorce you from life or from your experience and responsibilities here, but places you squarely within them, but with a greater purpose and a greater incentive.

We call the part of you that is not separated from God, Knowledge. We call it Knowledge because it is related to your ability to profoundly know things—beyond evidence, beyond reason, beyond normal calculations. You have the ability to see, to know and to act with the greater Intelligence of Knowledge as your guide and counsel. It is this Knowledge that will redeem you.

THE POWER OF KNOWLEDGE

God does not have to perseverate over your life and all your little affairs. The Lord of all the universes is not going to come and to attend to your life and be obsessed with your day-to-day difficulties and activities.

But God has placed within you the power of redemption. For Knowledge is the part of you that is wise and uncorrupted by the world, the part of you that is not afraid of the world. It is here to guide that part of you that *is* corrupted by the world, that *is* afraid of the world, and that has created a complex and often ineffective adaptation to the world.

Here Knowledge is meant to guide your mind—your intellect, your personal mind, your worldly mind—and all that it contains. It is Knowledge that will set a new course for you and bring different kinds of relationships into your life, re-establish your priorities and over time give you the eyes to see and the ears to hear.

This is such a phenomenal gift. It truly is a great endowment. But, of course, most people are too busy, too distracted and too obsessed with their own thinking and affairs to be able to experience Knowledge, or even be aware of it.

Some people call it intuition, those momentary flashes of insight or recognition that seem remarkable. But they are so rare and so infrequent and so unreliable that most people do not realize they actually have a greater Intelligence within them.

As the world grows more dark and difficult, as uncertainty arises, as the economic and social instability increases and the world braces itself for the Great Waves of change, the part of you that is weak will become more exasperated and more afraid. It will tend to enter into

LIVING IN SEPARATION

greater forms of denial and self-obsession to protect itself from the realities existing around it.

But into these increasingly difficult times, the power and the presence of Knowledge can emerge strongly because you will come to a point when you realize you need it; you must have it; you require its wisdom, its clarity, its integrity and its fearlessness.

God has planted Knowledge within every person as the seed and source of their redemption. Redemption will not occur because you believe in a great saint or a great Messenger. Redemption will not even occur if you believe in God or practice a religion faithfully, for you are still lost in the mind, the worldly mind. Your attempt at religion is an escape from the world, a desperate attempt to have purpose and meaning in your life that transcends the hard realities that you see all around you.

Yet real redemption occurs because you are responding to something powerful on the inside, and it is opening your mind to a greater realm of experience and relationships. It is transforming your perception and your idea of yourself.

This can take place whether you practice a religion or not. But religious practice can be very helpful here if you understand that is its purpose. Regardless of your tradition or the history of your tradition, the purpose of your practice is to engage you with the power and the presence of Knowledge.

Prayer, meditation, prostration, dedication, recitation, contemplation—these are all to bring you to this greater Intelligence that exists beyond the realm and the reach of the intellect. This is where you connect with God and where God can influence your thinking and behavior.

THE POWER OF KNOWLEDGE

Knowledge is not the subconscious mind. You cannot use it to gain wealth or advantage or to win people over. It is not like this at all. Your subconscious mind is still your worldly mind. It just has parts of it that you are unaware of or do not utilize on a daily basis.

We are speaking of something else—something more mysterious and profound, something you cannot use to enrich yourself. You cannot manipulate it because it is pure. It is more powerful than your intellect, your plans, your goals and your schemes. To think that you could use Knowledge to get what you want is to underestimate what Knowledge really is and to overestimate your abilities and your own wisdom to know what is true and right to do.

God redeems the separated through Knowledge, whether you are a human being living in this world or another intelligent being living in another world—in any world, in all worlds. For all sentient beings have Knowledge. This does not mean that they know of Knowledge or follow Knowledge or are aware of Knowledge, but it is there nonetheless.

Here you must turn your approach inward, for believing in Jesus or Muhammad or the Buddha will not bridge the gap of Separation that exists between you and your Source, and between the part of you that lives in the world and is of the world and the part of you that is not of the world.

Here Separation is both internal and external. In Separation, you are divorced from your deeper nature. It is unknown to you. It is a mystery. You are divorced from others. And you are seemingly divorced from your Source because that part of your mind that is worldly, living in Separation, actually thinks Separation is the real

LIVING IN SEPARATION

reality, it is the essence of things, it is the truth of things, it is the inescapable fact of things on a practical level.

You still have to function in the world. You still have to compete with others. You still have to get along with others. You have to deal with disagreement, dishonesty, conflict and all the machinations of the mind within yourself and within others.

Without Knowledge, this becomes so problematic and so hazardous and so unfortunate that people escape into fantasies and, if they can afford it, into hobbies and dreams to try to have some sense of value and meaning, some sense of permanence and reprieve from the world.

God's New Revelation presents The Way of Knowledge, as it is taught not only in this world, but throughout the Greater Community of worlds in the universe. It is a universal teaching. It is not overlaid with human history, human culture, human conflict or human personalities. It is essential and pure. It is the pathway the great mystics have always followed, the great artists, the great inventors, the great humanitarians. The evidence is in your history and in your world, but it is not mundane; it is not everywhere. You may have to search for it to find the inspiration in other people that is the evidence of a greater Knowledge at work.

To become truly honest, you must recognize your predicament and come to terms with it—without denial, without avoidance and without manipulation. Your predicament is you are living in Separation, and you are a stranger to yourself.

You know your tendencies and aspects of personality. You know something about your past. You know what you look like. You can

THE POWER OF KNOWLEDGE

distinguish yourself from others based upon qualities of your personality, activities and perhaps unique features.

But you are a stranger to your deeper nature, your real nature, your permanent nature—the part of you that has never left God and Creation, the part of you that lives within you today and that will be there for you when you leave this world, as it was there for you before you entered this world.

Without Knowledge, life is difficult. It is fearful. It is problematic. Though beautiful, it is also dangerous. Though pleasant, it is very painful. Great disappointment will attend you as your ideals fail and as you are disappointed by yourself and other people.

God knows this is the source of your suffering, your anxiety and your dysfunction. People do not realize this yet. They think they are doing well. They have advantages. They are moving forward. They have things other people do not have. Perhaps they live in a rich nation and have affluence and opportunity and food, water and energy are not a big problem.

But the condition is still the same, you see, whether you are the richest person on Earth or the poorest person living in the poorest country. Your circumstances are vastly different. Your opportunities are vastly different. The degree of social power you have is vastly different. But your predicament in Separation is still the same. You are still isolated and struggling in a world that does not seem to care very much about you.

This is a harsh reckoning, but a necessary one because this is where you become really honest with yourself. But to face this great truth, you must have the awareness of Knowledge, or you will become

46

LIVING IN SEPARATION

angry and jaded, negative and pessimistic. All hope will seem to leave you because you do not know the source of hope, the meaning of hope and where true inspiration comes from.

You may be entertained by the world and try to keep yourself in a state of entertainment through art and music, comedy and all of these things—if you can afford such things, which very few people can. But this is all an escape still, you see. Even working hard and priding yourself on your work accomplishments, even this becomes a form of escape.

People cannot sit still for five seconds. They are so driven and aggravated and obsessed. They are afraid of themselves. They are afraid of other people. They are afraid of life and what may come in the future. Driven they are, pathetic, and even more pathetic when they really have pride and think they are superior and above and beyond other people.

The Angels watch this and shake their heads: "This is truly a sad case. It will take longer for this person to come to terms with the reality of their life and situation."

In this respect, the rich are further from the truth than the poor. The rich are more caught up in their passions and obsessions, hobbies and activities. It can be more difficult for them to come to terms with the reality of their lives.

Into this hopeless situation, the Creator of all life has given the antidote—the antidote to suffering, the antidote to Separation. It lives mysteriously within you. You cannot use it and control it. You cannot extinguish it. You can avoid it and run from it, which you have been doing all along, but it is still there for you.

THE POWER OF KNOWLEDGE

God does not have to manage your life. God does not have to manage the affairs of this world. God does not control the weather and the sequence of events, for that is all in motion. That was set in motion at the beginning of time, and it is still in motion and will be in motion for as long as you can imagine.

The great redemption is the reclamation of Knowledge. God has provided the Steps to Knowledge, the preparation given with God's New Revelation. Here your thinking, intellectual mind, your worldly mind, is connected through practice, awareness and application to the deeper Mind of Knowledge within you.

Here it is important not to think that you already know of these things, that you are very intuitive, because you are only a beginner in The Way of Knowledge. Do not think that you have already traveled up and down this mountain, for you have never been on this mountain before.

It is all a question of honesty, you see. Honesty begins with what you tell yourself. Tell yourself a lie, and you will lie to others and think you are very consistent and are being honest. But you are merely spreading the dishonesty you have established with yourself, spreading it out into the world around you—misinforming others, creating false impressions. Even if you think you are being honest and want to be honest, until you have this deeper reckoning, dishonesty will still be a great problem for you.

Real honesty can be triggered by mishap in life, tragedy in life, loss in life. The benefit of these things is they can make you more honest and more able to reckon your real needs and circumstances.

LIVING IN SEPARATION

But you cannot resolve these things alone. You cannot resolve them based upon ideas or theories alone. You cannot base them on productive activities alone because you need the guidance of Knowledge.

To receive this guidance, you must yield to Knowledge. You must yield your preferences, your wishes and your obsessions. You cannot follow if you insist upon leading. Yet the act of following is the act of bridging the gap, and slowly and incrementally undoing Separation.

It is honesty that tells you if your relationship with another is real and genuine and has promise for the future. Regardless of attractions and beauty and charm, agreements and prior investments and all of this, it is honesty, self-honesty.

What motivates you to be this honest is that you do not want to suffer. You do not want to waste your life on a meaningless pursuit or a relationship that has no future or destiny. It is suffering that teaches you to value your experience and your time. It is suffering that can bring you back to yourself and to God.

Yet no one wants to suffer, so everyone tries to escape suffering in the pursuit of happiness and all of its manifestations. But it is disappointment that brings you back. It is sobriety that brings you back. It is reconciliation with yourself that brings you back. It is facing your mistakes and the loss of your time and life that brings you back.

Knowledge is waiting for you, but you must recognize your need for Knowledge. This is a fundamental and essential recognition. It is the beginning of real self-honesty and real honesty with others.

THE POWER OF KNOWLEDGE

Without Knowledge, you are constantly misrepresenting yourself and your intentions to others. You are trying to get things from people. You want to use them as resources. You want them for pleasure or security, companionship or advantage of some kind. So you do not see the meaning of the relationship or the lack of meaning of the relationship. You only see what you want out of the situation.

Here you misrepresent yourself, you become dishonest, you establish false expectations, false goals, false relationships, false involvements and so forth until you become entwined and lost in a set of circumstances that you can no longer control. You have given your life away. You have cast your fate. Now you must live with the consequences. And the journey out of that jungle is very difficult and very trying.

You must come to your need for Knowledge. In a moment of real sobriety and self-honesty, you will see that you cannot find your way without Knowledge. You cannot resolve your dilemmas without Knowledge. You cannot know who you are without Knowledge. You cannot discern the true relationships from the false without Knowledge. You cannot bridge to a new and better life without Knowledge. You cannot resolve the problems of the world without Knowledge.

You may come to this realization incrementally. You may come in moments of sobriety and self-examination. You may come in moments of disappointment and disillusionment. Perhaps the realization will happen gradually, step by step, as you learn to take the Steps to Knowledge.

People begin this journey thinking that Knowledge is going to be a resource for them. They are going to use Knowledge to get what they

LIVING IN SEPARATION

want—better work, better relationships, better health, better opportunities, better advantages, more pleasure and less pain. But at some point they must come to see that Knowledge is not really going to give them what they want. It is really here to provide them what they truly need and what they desire at a deeper, more profound level.

People do not see this at the outset because they are not yet honest enough to recognize their truest and most profound needs. They are still trying to play life for advantages, to maneuver in life for advantages, to play the hazardous game for advantages. They have not yet come to a place of honesty and humility to see that they need God's Guidance and Power in their life, and without it—though they may try bravely to navigate a difficult world and to resolve complex and seemingly pervasive problems—they will not really be able to be successful.

It is in giving up illusions that you bring yourself to this moment of recognition. Here you begin to take the Steps to Knowledge with real intention. It is not merely a wonderful thing to do to enhance your life, to sweeten your life, to give you advantages, to make you look more spiritual to yourself. It is here to actually save you, to redeem you, to restore you, to renew you, to give you a greater authority within yourself and a true sense of integrity. Knowledge connects you with your deeper conscience, not your social conscience, but your deeper conscience that was created by God.

It is teaching spirituality at the level of Knowledge that is part of God's New Revelation for the world. Though the teaching in Knowledge is present in all of the world's religions, it has been lost and obscured by history and ritual and intellectual debate,

THE POWER OF KNOWLEDGE

adaptation to societies and the manipulation and use by governments.

Here The Way of Knowledge is plainly presented—purely, simply, directly. It is no longer obscure, but essential. For all religions are pathways to Knowledge because Knowledge is how God redeems you, and how you end the Separation within yourself, and between yourself and others, and between yourself and your Source.

This is a great journey. It is called by many names, but it is the great journey. It is the freedom journey. It is the most essential pursuit and the most essential relationship in life.

Knowledge is your primary relationship because it is your connection to God. Here you connect to God not through belief or through fervent spiritual practice. You connect to God by following what God wants you to do and by receiving what God is giving you to restore and to redeem your life.

Therefore, begin the journey. Take the Steps to Knowledge. Realize that you cannot find your way without this greater power and presence to guide you. Be patient, for the journey is long. Knowledge is mysterious. It does not come upon demand. It is not something you can control and manipulate. You must come into its presence in humility, with patience and openness, watching for the signs, and learning how to sincerely ask for guidance.

All of this is based upon your self-awareness and your self-honesty. It is so essential. It is not complex. It is not elusive if you approach it honestly. It is foremost and essential in your life. And that is why it is the greatest and most essential relationship.

LIVING IN SEPARATION

For God will guide you and protect you through Knowledge. God will redeem you and restore you through Knowledge. It is through Knowledge that you will discover over time your greater purpose for being in the world and those essential relationships that can make the expression and the fulfillment of this purpose possible.

CHAPTER 5

THE CRISIS

As revealed to
Marshall Vian Summers
on May 8, 2015
in London, United Kingdom

Behind all the pleasantries you see in the world, and the appearance
of happiness and success, and the appearance of contentment, there
is the crisis, the crisis within the person, within each person, within
you—a crisis that is always there until it is resolved; a crisis you carry
with you into all of your activities and relationships; a crisis that
haunts you and keeps you living apart from yourself, running away
from your deeper experience, hiding out in the world somewhere,
hiding out in religion, hiding out in politics, hiding out in hobbies or
pastimes. It is because of the crisis that this is the case.

People keep themselves stimulated all the time, or attempt to,
because they do not want to feel the crisis. It is this crisis, you see, of
being lost in the world, of living in Separation from your Source and
all that is permanent within you and around you. Cast out, escaped
you are, into a situation where you do not know what you are
doing—ever afraid of the environment, ever afraid of change, ever
afraid of loss and destruction. So in the world you see people are
trying all manner of escape from this.

Yet the crisis is not merely poverty or oppression. That is a crisis
at another level. But We are speaking of something much more
fundamental—the crisis that plagues the rulers of nations as well
as the citizens at every level of society. It is this crisis.

55

THE POWER OF KNOWLEDGE

You cannot settle this crisis on your own. The pain of Separation is with you. The confusion of Separation is with you. The fear and anxiety of Separation are with you. You may tell yourself anything. You may believe in anything. You may try to live out your dreams and fantasies, your preferences and your desires, but you carry the crisis with you. It is always with you until it can be resolved.

But God has put an answer within you to resolve the crisis, to set out a pathway to end the state of Separation, to give you a greater purpose, meaning and value in the world so that your journey here can truly be meaningful and represent your real nature and purpose here.

For belief cannot do this alone. Adhering to a religious principle or system of belief alone cannot do this, cannot resolve the crisis.

It is not just a crisis of faith. It is the crisis that even requires faith. For if you must have faith, it means you are already distant from your Source. You are not experiencing the power of Knowledge that God has put within you, so you must have faith. Without the crisis, there is no need for faith. Faith then is the evidence of the crisis. Faith is armor against the crisis.

But when faith fails you, and there will be times when it will fail you, you will feel the crisis—a complete sense of being lost and disassociated, of being fearful and apart from yourself, apart from your Source, apart from others. It is a kind of Hell, you see, that lives within you, that you carry with you until it can be resolved.

God understands the crisis. It is the crisis of Separation. Everyone who enters the physical reality is entering Separation, now attempting to live as an individual, now attempting to fulfill oneself,

THE CRISIS

if that is even possible given the lack of freedom there is in the universe.

It is your condition living in the physical reality. It is not your eternal state. It is not the state you have come from and to which you will return eventually. But it is your state living in time and space, limited by a body, governed by a mind, governed by the mind that is a product of living in this environment.

If you can begin to see that there is a crisis within you that you have been avoiding and running away from as far back as you can remember, you will see that there is a great need of your soul to be relieved of this—a need so deep, a need so ever present, regardless of your circumstances. Regardless of whether you are alone or married to another, regardless of who you are with, there is the crisis.

When you can begin to see this, and feel this, and have the honesty to look back into your life, to see what you are really afraid of, a fear that is even greater than the fear of death or loss, the fear of this crisis, then you will see and begin to see the deeper need of your soul—the need to reunite with your Source, not simply to ask God for favors or dispensations or to rescue you from your predicaments, but to reunite with your Source while you are here.

For without your Source, you are lost, no matter how firm your beliefs or how controlling you attempt to be over your circumstances and the opinions of others. That is why it is often in times of great disappointment or loss that people really begin to feel this deeper state and need. It is not pleasant by any means. It is not a desirable thing to deal with, but it represents your core reality.

THE POWER OF KNOWLEDGE

But God has given the answer. The answer was given at the beginning of time, at the beginning of the Separation. For living in Separation, you lose contact with the deeper part of you that has never been apart from God. But you have not lost this, you see. So your relief from the crisis is guaranteed. It is only a matter of time. It is only a matter of you gaining the honesty and self-awareness you need to see your situation very clearly.

God's New Revelation for the world reveals this crisis and speaks of it very clearly, with great compassion, with great love. For there is no anger or vengeance in God. That is a human creation. That is the product of living in Separation. That is a response to the crisis We speak of here today.

God has given you something important to do in life. The awareness of this is within Knowledge within you, deep beneath the surface of the mind that you think with currently. It is not merely a recognition or an awareness because you must do things in life to restore your dignity, to restore your value, not to prove this to God, but to prove it to yourself. You must earn back your self-respect, your self-trust and your self-love.

God knows you are living in Separation and without Knowledge you can only be in error, that you will live a life of desperation and fear, with great dangers all around you and within you. There is no condemnation here.

The crisis is trying to live without your Source and your Sacred Community that exist beyond the visible range. It is trying to be alone. But you are never really alone. It is a greater delusion, a tragic misunderstanding.

58

THE CRISIS

All the damage you see in the world—human cruelty, human violence against oneself and others, human degradation, human addiction—is all a product of this crisis. Even if you live the most upstanding life, even if you are highly regarded, the crisis is still there.

We bring this forth because it must be understood in a true light. The great discomfort you feel within yourself, the restlessness you feel within yourself, the need for constant stimulation and outer engagement, demonstrate this crisis and its reality for you.

That is why people are afraid to be still. That is why people are afraid to face themselves. They do not want to feel what they really feel. And they fear that if they face this, it will overtake them and consume them and destroy them.

But God has put Knowledge within you, the perfect antidote to the crisis. For there is a place within you that is wise and compassionate, that is uncorrupted by the world. It is not the product of belief or religious affiliation. It is the gift of your Creator, a gift that you carry with you in your journey in the physical universe. It is here to restore you and to relieve you of your burden, to bring resolution to your dilemma, which you yourself cannot resolve.

To turn towards your Source knowing your great need is the most primary thing you could do. Do not wait until you are on your deathbed to do this. Do not bring calamity upon your outer life to bring you to this point. Do not degrade your life or fall into dissolution in order to have this recognition.

Your sorrow will be replaced with great confidence and great appreciation. Your anxiety will be replaced by the desire to

THE POWER OF KNOWLEDGE

participate in a world you have come to serve. Your enthusiasm will replace your lack of self-trust. Your authority will give you strength. And your humility will enable you to serve.

God has given you a way out of the jungle. God has given you the resolution to the crisis. But you must live the resolution. You must act upon it. It is not merely a moment of self-realization.

You must serve because that is why you have come. That is the purpose God has given you—a very specific purpose to give in a certain way, to certain people and situations. You are perfectly designed for this.

You do not heal the crisis by having a new understanding or a better point of view or a spiritual answer for everything. It is embarking on a new life guided by Knowledge that brings the great resolution to your life.

Now your life is not based on fear and preference, and a desperate attempt to satisfy your unquenchable thirst for excitement or avoidance. The deeper pain within you can only be resolved by the gift of purpose and meaning that Knowledge within you carries for you, waiting to be discovered.

To live a life of compassion and service is something that is so remarkable. Yet you will still suffer for the conditions of the world, you will fear for the safety of others, and you will have trials and difficulty along the way. But that is life itself here. The difference is that the crisis will be over within you, not all at once, but incrementally as you continue to follow the true and clear path.

THE CRISIS

You must demonstrate the greater life to others and to yourself. It is you who must be convinced. Those who watch over you know who you are, but you do not know this yet.

The crisis will fall away bit by bit, lose intensity, lose its strength, lose its grip upon you as you proceed—following a greater purpose and calling in the world. That part of you that is strong will lead that part of you that is weak as you make progress here.

This is the proper use of time. Otherwise, time is kind of a curse, you see, because you do not have much of it, and yet it seems to go on forever and be never ending. Time is your problem, in a way, because you are losing ground. The longer you fail to respond to the power that is within you, the more you are losing ground—the weaker you are becoming.

Even as you acquire all things in the world and seem to have great prestige and admiration from others, you are still pathetic. You are still in trouble. You are still unknown to yourself. And your greater purpose and calling are unknown to you.

We are like the physician who is telling you that you have a problem you do not want to admit having. You would rather live in denial because you are accustomed to that. But the physician is not here to tell you how great your life is, but to show you where you are suffering, where your life is in danger and imperiled, and can degrade your experience and your existence here.

While there is a crisis within you, there is a crisis in the world, growing now to ever-greater proportions. That is why you also have come, to play your small but important part in meeting that crisis. It is not merely that you get to be relieved of your pain and your

THE POWER OF KNOWLEDGE

difficulty in life. That would not be enough, you see. But that is not why you have come, really. You have come to deal with the great crisis of the world, the great change in the world's environment, the great upheaval in nations and societies facing a changing world. You have come for this.

It is in meeting this [greater] crisis that your crisis can be resolved, but only if you are following the power of Knowledge that God has given to you. Otherwise, you will be a warrior. You will be an advocate only. But your problem is still unrecognized and unresolved. It is meeting the inner and outer problem together that creates the true resolution on both fronts, in both realities, within you and beyond you.

You cannot return to your Heavenly Home with the crisis. It must be undone here, for it was created here. It must be resolved here, for it was established here.

So even when you leave this life, if you have completed your work here, you will serve those who remain behind—those of your own world, your own kind—because you must help them be relieved of their crisis. Your success must now be the gift to others.

It is this giving born of resolution, born of purpose, born of meaning, born of the power and grace of Knowledge that God has put within you that will be an ongoing contribution in your life, in your time and in the times to come beyond this life and this time.

So in the end, there is not even a fragment of the crisis left. There is no residue left. It has all been flushed out of you because your life was moving in a true direction. You have become integrated with Knowledge. You have become yourself, finally.

THE CRISIS

There is no human therapy that can end the crisis. It may make you aware of the crisis. It may help you deal with the crisis. But it cannot resolve it. For that you need a Higher Power. You need the power of Knowledge within you, born of God. And you need God's Grace and the Angelic Assembly that watches over the world. You need great assistance.

But down here on the ground, you will have to do the work. You will have to face the change that must be brought about in your circumstances and in your agreements and associations with others. And you must face the consequences of this. You must be the architect of your new life. You must make mistakes and correct them. You must gain wisdom and strength. There is no escaping this. Without this, your dignity would not be restored. Your value would not be restored. The purpose and meaning of your life would not be restored or realized.

That is why God does not just sweep away your problems. For God did not create your problems. Yet God has given you the power to resolve them and to bring your life into its true harmony and balance here in service to the great change that is coming, in service to the world facing this great change.

You and others are called into the world at this time to face the great upheaval, to contribute and to protect human civilization. For much has been done to contribute to this world from Heaven above, and facing great trial now, great danger, many are sent here to serve.

Do not think you are apart from this. You know so little about who you are, where you have come from and who has sent you here. That is part of your crisis. You know so little about where your life is destined to go and where it can be of the greatest value and meaning.

THE POWER OF KNOWLEDGE

And that is part of your crisis. You know so little about your origin and your destiny beyond this world. And that is part of your crisis.

But the problem that seems to have no answer has an answer. God's New Revelation for the world presents this very clearly, more clearly than it has ever been presented in this world, presented now to a literate world, to a world of global communication and growing global awareness, given now so it can reach many people everywhere—in every religion, in every nation, in every culture.

The Messenger is in the world to receive and to present God's New Revelation, which has come at the critical turning point for humanity, a turning point that will determine the fate and the future of every person and all who are yet to come.

Surely, the importance of this outshines anything that you think is important. Clearly, the need is greater than any need that you can understand. Clearly, to be sent into the world at such a time is of immense importance.

Face this and you will realize you have work to do. It is the unfinished business of your life. It is the one thing that can restore you and free you from the crisis.

Failure here has great consequence. Your life will be forfeited. It will be empty. The world will not be served. Your gifts will not be given where they were meant to be given. And when you return to your Spiritual Family, you will see very clearly that you did not make the connection. There will be no condemnation there, but there will be the perfect Knowledge that you must return and try again.

THE CRISIS

For in that state, you will remember that you were sent into the world, why you were sent and what the world needs. You will remember what you cannot yet see in this moment because your mind is taken up with other things, dominated by other things— things on the outside, things on the inside.

But God has put the answer within you, and it goes with you every moment of every day. And it is constantly seeking to drive you and take you and move you in the true direction of your life, to free you from dangerous and unfulfilling circumstances, to set your life on a new course, step by step. You may pray to God for many things, but God has already given you the ultimate gift.

May this power and presence strike you, gain your attention, let you feel the pain that is within you and yet remind you there is a way out.

You must face yourself in this regard to see the great need of your soul, to see the great need of your life, to see that you cannot resolve this on your own. No worldly power can resolve this. No worldly pleasure or wealth can resolve this.

The degree to which you can do this is important. And your ability to respond to God's New Revelation is very important. It means there is great promise for you if you can respond and take the Steps to Knowledge that have been provided, and begin to honor yourself and others, and see the great cost of Separation all around you—with clear eyes, without condemnation.

It is the pain of your life and of the world that will finally turn you to your Source, in humility and honesty, seeking that which alone can resolve the great dilemma that exists within you and all around you.

CHAPTER 6

THE PRESENCE

As revealed to
Marshall Vian Summers
on December 7, 2009
in Chau Doc, Vietnam

People are very busy, very stimulated, rushing about always, unable
to be still, unable to listen within themselves, the mind restless,
always searching, full of passion, full of fear, full of persuasions, full
of denial.

Why is this so? Why are such intelligent creatures such as human
beings so driven, so anxious and so uncontented? Why is this the
case with nearly everyone?

People speak of a spiritual reality. People speak of God. People speak
of Heaven and Hell. People speak of their faith. But they are still
restless, uneasy, confused.

Why is this so, that even with an awareness that one has a deeper
nature, that there should be this uneasiness?

The answer is really deeper than most people would suspect and
more confusing than people would think.

For so close to you is the Presence, but if you cannot be with this
Presence, then where will you go? What will you do? How can you
avoid being with something that is so ever present, that is within you
and around you?

THE POWER OF KNOWLEDGE

It would seem to be inescapable, and yet people do not experience it. You would think it would be ever present, but it remains unknown. Even amongst those who claim to be religious and inspired and guided, it is a foreign experience. And if they do experience it, it is only for moments at a time.

If you cannot be with something that is ever present within you and around you, then how will you escape this? Where will you go where the Presence is not with you?

It is a dilemma and a mystery, and the answer seems mysterious as well. It is the contradiction of living in manifest reality that a spiritual Being would be apparently so unspiritual—groveling like an animal, driven by external forces, kept to such a low point in a struggle to live.

Surely, even the most optimistic person will hit these low points of experience, and if they are honest with themselves, they are feeling things within themselves that are hardly admirable or desirable. But that which is not admirable, that which is undesirable, are not part of the Presence, for it is pure.

If someone sits still long enough and is able to quiet their mind, they will begin to feel the Presence. If someone begins to feel their real state of being, the real condition of their mind and their body, and they are able to be with themselves at a deeper level, they will begin to feel the Presence.

When people honestly give to another without the desire for self-enrichment or self-validation, they feel the Presence. When you are moved by inspiration by the action of another, you feel the Presence.

THE PRESENCE

It is so close. Strip away the veneer of human psychology, and there is the Presence.

What is this Presence? And why is it so ever present? It is the presence of your Spiritual Family. It is the presence of Creation. It is the Presence of the Source of all these things because you never left God. You did not physically leave God from one place and go to another place where God did not exist because there is no place where God does not exist. God is omnipresent. God even exists in Hell, or in states of mind that are hellish.

It must be a real problem to avoid God. Yet people are doing this. Not even knowing why they are doing this, they are doing this.

When you leave this life, when your body passes away, it is not like you disappear and go somewhere else. You just awaken to what has always been there. There are those who sent you into the world, waiting to greet you. And there is the Presence, the magnificent Presence. You did not journey from one place to another to experience this. It was always there.

So why do people resist this? Why do they attempt to avoid it at all costs? Why do they seek a worldly experience of suffering and struggle and constant adaptation when they could experience the Presence?

It is a question that is haunting, and yet its answer is an experience itself—the desire to experience this Presence, the intent of stopping oneself from one's desperate thinking and behavior, the desire to experience one's real nature and purpose in the world—a turning point within the individual.

69

THE POWER OF KNOWLEDGE

Instead of running away, instead of trying to keep yourself in a state of fantasy, in a state of aggravation, you decide that you do not want these things anymore, and you are willing to go through a process of coming back to the Presence.

The reason you do not experience the Presence is it is hidden—hidden by the appearance of the world, hidden by the make-up of your mind, hidden by your circumstances and by your focus in life. Like the sleeping person who sleeps in paradise, but dreams of Hell, unaware that beyond their sleeping state, they are in a place of grace and meaning.

You have invested so much to be in the world, to invest in your identity here. You have built so much resistance to your original state by being here, you do not want anything that will bring that to an end. That is partly why people are afraid to die.

But We are not talking about dying. We are talking about waking up. We are talking about taking away the layers and layers of deception and obsession, all that you have placed over the light, all the world has placed over the light, until the light has disappeared and is seen no more.

It is like your mind and body have become the shade of the lamp, but the shade is so dark and overlaying that the light does not penetrate through. Instead of casting this light upon the world, it remains hidden within you. It remains hidden in almost everyone.

Part of the reason that people do not want to feel the Presence is it casts in doubt everything that they are attempting to have, to be and to do. It casts in doubt the reality of Separation itself.

70

THE PRESENCE

If God is right there, if Creation is right there, even your Spiritual Family, whom you barely remember, is right there, then what is this reality you are experiencing in the world? How real is it? How important is it?

This begins a kind of revolution within yourself, a revolution with opposing forces—the desire to awaken and to experience the Presence and the fear of the Presence, and the fear of the pain that the Presence would reveal, the fear of the discord and conflict that the Presence would reveal, the fear of recognition that your life is empty and that your goals are questionable.

Then there is the fear of God—the fear that you have denied God and that God will punish you, the fear that you have been sinful and bad and that God and God's claimed wrath and displeasure will somehow come down upon you. People think there is a Judgment Day, and they certainly do not want it to be today.

This is the whole problem with Separation because it requires the denial of Creation. To live in the reality of Separation requires the denial of Creation because Creation is of God. It is not these physical things that you touch and sense. It is far beyond that.

When you begin to experience the Presence, it begins to draw you. It is the most natural attraction there can be. Of course, you want to experience it more, particularly when you find out it is not there to punish you, when you find out it is not full of judgment and wrath and displeasure, when you find out that it is wondrous and magnificent.

Of course you would want to return to it. What else in the world can give you this experience? Here you do not leave the world, but

THE POWER OF KNOWLEDGE

instead discover you have a greater purpose for being here, a natural memory, a deeper sense. It follows the experience of the Presence, and this precedes the experience of the Presence.

But it is a conscious decision to turn one's life, to shift direction, to go against the great investment in Separation, to go against one's fear, to go against one's desire that keeps leading you into the world—trying to lose yourself there; trying to create a new identity there; trying to be, do and have things there.

Here you do not give up everything and become an ascetic, unless you have a special calling to do that. For most people, it really represents having their life being illuminated and informed and going through a great transition—internally a great transition and a great transition on the outside. Because if you feel the Presence, or at least are aware that it is there watching you, that will change your life and your goals and your priorities and everything.

Even the reality that God is watching you is unnerving to people. It is unnerving because they are trying to hide. Like the little creature that wants to hide under a rock, it does not want to be discovered, fearing it will be destroyed. This is how people regard God. Even if they believe in God, they do not want to experience God today because that seems to be the end of everything. "Believe in God today, and you can be with God later, but not today, please—not ready for God."

That is why being religious is no guarantee that you will experience the Presence or the greater purpose that has brought you here to the world. These discoveries can be made by the person who has no religion or does not even believe in religion. Sometimes belief in religion can even make this fundamental discovery even more difficult because of the belief in retribution and the belief in a

THE PRESENCE

Judgment Day and the belief in Hell. No one wants to confront these things. Not today. Not any day.

So We come back to the original question of why people are in avoidance. They do not want to think that God is watching them and that the Presence is right there, looking at all of their thoughts and their behavior, all of their misdeeds, all of their licentiousness, all of their violent thinking, all of their resentments and their grievances and the terrible things that pass through their imagination.

But God is not appalled by these things, for God is focused on you—not the you that you have created in Separation, but the you that God created, that is part of Creation itself.

What We are speaking of here is at the very heart of the human dilemma. And it is not just a human dilemma, it is a dilemma of all manifest intelligent life in the universe and even in other universes.

Other races in the universe, though they may appear to be different from you, and even those who have greater technology are still facing the fundamental problem of Separation. The Presence is with them too, but they cannot feel it. They do not want it. And in most cases, they do not even believe it is there.

So what is the value of all these things you seek in the world—comfort, security, pleasure, power, wealth—if they rob you of your Divine connection, if they obliterate your awareness of the Presence and with it your greater purpose for being in this world at this time?

People have moments where they look at things a little more objectively and they think, "Hmm. These things that everyone is clamoring for and desiring, are they really that important?" They

73

THE POWER OF KNOWLEDGE

have moments of introspection. Perhaps following times of disappointment or disillusionment, they have moments of introspection—hopeful moments, reconsidering moments.

It is not about religion. It is not about saviors. It is not about what faith tradition you belong to. It is about the Presence. It is not about your ideology or what religious system you might adhere to.

People ask all the wrong questions, you see. The emphasis is all wrong. They think it is all about ideas. They think it is about the allegiance to your ideas because they live in a world of ideas. It is really about the Presence—not an evil presence, not a deceiving presence, but the real Presence.

There are evil presences. There are deceiving presences. There are dark presences, oh yes, but We are speaking of the real Presence. What is a dark presence, but a shadow upon the landscape, when the real Presence is the light that illuminates the entire landscape?

If you were to experience this Presence more consistently, you would begin to feel and to experience that you have a greater presence and purpose in the world, a greater direction to follow that does not have much to do with your former goals and aspirations.

It would require you to reconsider everything you are doing—reconsider all of your relationships, except perhaps with your children, for whom you would have to maintain a responsible position as a provider. You would have to reconsider everything you are doing. People do not seem to want to do that. It is the small price you pay for revelation, and oh, what a small price it is compared to what is being revealed here.

THE PRESENCE

God has sent a New Message into the world revealing the power of the Presence. God has provided a pathway through the study of Steps to Knowledge. God has revealed the real nature of your spiritual reality at the level of Knowledge, the deeper Intelligence within you. It is all aimed to bring you to the Presence, and then to bring you to your greater purpose in the world, which lives deep within you and which has been with you all along.

When We speak of you returning to the Presence, We do not mean returning completely because if you did that, you could not be in the world. You would lose all desire and intention for being here because the Presence is so powerful and has such great appeal.

No, God only wants you to experience a little of the Presence—enough to enable you to stop your self-destructive thinking and behavior, enough to engage you with your deeper reality, enough to give you the courage to face and to reconsider your life and circumstances, enough for you to experience the power and the presence of Knowledge within yourself and have the courage and the desire to follow it above all other things in life.

The purpose is not to return to God. First, you must fulfill your mission and destiny in the world and re-enter the world of pain and difficulty, of confusion and contrast, but now with a greater reality guiding you.

So you have a taste of the Presence and many tastes of the Presence, but you cannot go there entirely because that would take you out of the world. God wants you to be in the world, and you have the perfect Knowledge that you need to be here—not to lose yourself in Separation, not to try to recreate yourself, not to try to make

THE POWER OF KNOWLEDGE

Separation successful, but to experience and to fulfill a greater destiny here.

It is as if you have two purposes for being in the world. You have a personal purpose of escaping into a world of Separation. But God has sent with you a greater purpose for contribution in the world, and this goes with you everywhere.

So as it is true you cannot escape the Presence, you also cannot escape the greater purpose that has brought you here. It goes everywhere with you too. But your dilemma is how are you going to experience these things within yourself and go through the natural transition and change in your priorities and sense of direction that these will indicate?

To awaken from a life of addiction requires that you give up that life, and people do not want to give up their previous investment. People just want to be happy in their previous investment. But they can never be happy there even though they keep trying.

You cannot make an old life work. You need a new life. Even if you remain in most of your current circumstances, you still need a new life. The Revelation gives you a new life. God's New Message for the world gives you new life. Even the great religious traditions of the world can give you new life if you can understand them correctly and not be dissuaded by many of the errors in thinking that exist there.

People keep trying to make their life work when their life just does not work. They keep trying to make their circumstances appealing and acceptable to their deeper nature, but their deeper nature has other plans. They try to believe in God, but do not want God to

76

THE PRESENCE

appear that day. They pray for guidance and deliverance, but they are afraid of guidance and deliverance.

This is the dilemma of Separation. It is a dilemma that is so fundamental to your being in the world and to the confusion you experience about yourself, your place and your purpose here, a sense of confusion that permeates your relationships and your activities.

That is why in God's New Revelation, as in God's older Revelations and previous Revelations, there is always this emphasis on returning to God—not worshipping God from afar, not simply believing, but opening the door within yourself to an inner revelation, which translates into the experience of the Presence, and the discovery that one has a greater purpose, and the desire and the ability to go through a great revolution within yourself that allows you to realize this purpose and to follow it and then to re-apply yourself in the world.

The Presence will draw you, but it will also send you back. It will give you a new life over time, but it will send you back. There is no running away to God because that is not your purpose for being in the world—your real purpose. But you need God or the Presence to recognize this real purpose and to find the courage to follow it.

Even if you are not a religious person and do not think in religious terms, it all amounts to the same thing—a deep inner conviction, a deep inner conscience, a deep inner motivation, a sense of what is right and a deep sense of what is not right that seems to go beyond one's political views or social attitudes, a deeper conscience not shaped by your culture and society and family—a deeper conscience that was established in your creation long before you came to this world.

THE POWER OF KNOWLEDGE

So in the study of Steps to Knowledge, you learn to be still—not so you can get information, not so you can have the winning number, not so you can be more clever and more cunning in life, but to experience the Presence.

First, you will experience the presence of your Teachers standing around you, those who are sent to overlook your life and other lives. They exist beyond the physical realm, and you will experience their presence, which is very powerful. But that will lead you to a greater experience of Presence as your desire and capacity for the Presence increases.

The Presence is so overwhelming that when you first experience it, it is like a momentary flash of light, like a flash of lightning illuminating the landscape at night. For a brief second, you can see everything, and then it is all dark again. You had a moment of experiencing the Presence, but it was only a moment because you really do not have yet the desire or the capacity for that experience to grow. That has to be developed through practice and intention. Steps to Knowledge has many steps to take you through this, to give you time to build this desire for the Presence and your capacity to experience it, which is fundamentally a capacity to experience relationship.

You see, your capacity to experience relationship determines the quality of your relationship with others. If you have extremely limited capacity, that will limit your experience of relationship with others. This translates into your life directly and immediately. The more you experience the Presence, the more you can be with other people, the more you can be with yourself, the more you can be in life.

78

THE PRESENCE

The translation to the quality of your life is tremendous and natural. It has to happen. But at this point, you have to be convinced, you have to be lured by God, lured by the promise of peace and happiness and meaning, power and fulfillment because you are so afraid, so afraid that God might appear one day and redirect your life.

Yet that is what you want. Part of you wants it. Part of you does not. Part of you seeks the relationship. Part of you will run away from it. So it is working this out that represents the process of revelation.

Revelation just is not a big sensational moment. It is a process of returning. It has its illuminating moments, but it is a process in time—the most natural process there is.

Stop for a moment. Allow your mind to settle down. Breathe deeply. Go to a quiet place. Set aside your thoughts and your plans and goals and problems long enough, you do this frequently enough, and you begin to experience the Presence. After awhile, it just emerges, in small glimpses at first and then, as you proceed, you will have larger experiences of it, enough to show you what you need to see and know about yourself and about your circumstances.

This is the process of revelation. God's New Message for the world speaks of revelation in these terms. It is a Message for the world that is pure. It has not been corrupted by political forces or power-seeking individuals. It is something that is pure and elemental. It is meant for everyone.

It can illuminate your life if you approach it honestly and are willing to follow its recommendations. Your desire for this is the desire for the Presence. Your willingness for this is the willingness to experience the Presence and all that the Presence reveals. Your fear of this is your fear

THE POWER OF KNOWLEDGE

of the Presence. Your denial of this is your denial of the Presence. Whatever reasons you give for this denial are secondary and insignificant compared to the denial itself.

Not everyone is ready for their personal revelation. That is not your concern. Your concern is if you are ready, if you are ready to go through the process of revelation—a process of illumination, a process of change, a process of re-evaluation, a process of shifting your emphasis in life from Separation to union and relationship. You must think on these things, and keep thinking on these things, and never stop thinking on these things.

We are part of the Presence, the part that is here to guide you and to bring the New Message into the world. We are those who have achieved the ability to live beyond the limits of the world and the limits even of the body. And so We serve the purpose of all life because it is Our joy to do this.

Those like Us, who represent the Plan of the Divine, they too will assist you as you begin this process of revelation. They will encourage you without taking control of your life. For you must take control of your life, guided by Knowledge.

There is so much to learn and unlearn that anything We say can be misconstrued and used against the Revelation. But that is the risk that must be taken to bring this awareness to you and to encourage you to take the Steps to Knowledge, to receive God's New Message for the world, which is being given at a time of grave danger for humanity, a time of great change and upheaval. It is being given to people in all faith traditions to illuminate those traditions and to bring forth the essence of their Teachings so that everyone will have a chance to experience the Presence.

THE PRESENCE

The Presence is with you at this moment. It is standing right behind you. It is underneath the surface of your mind. It exists in everything you see and touch. Yet it permeates these things beyond your visible range. You experience the Presence with a deeper sense that goes beyond the senses of the body.

It is with you now. It was with you yesterday. And it will be with you tomorrow—calling you and waiting for your return; waiting to bestow upon you a life of purpose, meaning and direction; waiting for you to choose the path of revelation and to turn away from the darkness of your imagination and the fearful life that you are attempting to live.

Let this be your understanding.

CHAPTER 7

THE RECONCILIATION

As revealed to
Marshall Vian Summers
on May 2, 2011
in Boulder, Colorado

You are living in Separation—separate from Creation itself, separate from your Source, separate even from your deeper nature—living in a different part of your mind, a mind that has been shaped and conditioned by your experience of the world. You identify with your body and your ideas. You give yourself a name. You are distinct and seemingly distinguished from everyone around you. You are living in Separation.

You came into the world with a purpose, sent here by your Spiritual Family, a purpose to serve in a unique way within the circumstances of your life and the conditions of the world. So while you are living in a state of Separation, you are still connected to your Source. You are still connected to those who sent you into the world. You are still connected to Creation.

It is this contradiction within your own nature that is really what it means to be a human being. It is this contradiction that gives your life promise, for you have come for a greater purpose—a purpose that you did not invent, a purpose that you cannot really change, a purpose that your deeper nature is committed to at the level of your soul.

THE POWER OF KNOWLEDGE

If this were not the case, then you would be lost in the world. You would be a fragment of the physical universe. Your life would have no intrinsic meaning or value beyond the estimation of others with whom you are engaged. Life would seem to be empty and pointless. And whether you were rich or poor, regardless of your circumstances, the fact of your Separation would always haunt you, generating fear—fear of loss, fear of harm, fear of deprivation, fear of destruction.

It is this fear that governs people's lives, determining their decisions, overshadowing whatever little happiness they seem to create and try to create. It is the constant anxiety. It is the feelings of regret. It is the longing and the unfulfillment that is part of every person's experience of the world.

Yet the Separation was never really created. You cannot be separate from your Source, and that is why there is no Hell and damnation. There is only the process of reconciliation. No matter how long it takes, that is the end result. Your contradiction and your decision is what voice you will listen to within yourself.

For God has given you a deeper conscience—not a social conscience, but an intrinsic conscience that is part of the deeper Intelligence We call Knowledge. It is not confused. It is not conflicted. And it is not afraid of the world, for nothing can destroy it. The world can obscure it, overshadow it and take you away from it, but within itself, it is complete. It is the part of you that is part of Creation itself.

This is what will save you, you see. This is what is connected to God and to all who serve God—within this world and other worlds and beyond the physical reality itself. This exists beyond the realm of the intellect. It is something you must experience and express and apply

THE RECONCILIATION

in your life, and that is what will demonstrate its power, its reality and its efficacy.

You do not know who you are, regardless of your definitions or what you put on your nametag, but deeper down there is no question. Who you are in this world, in this life, is what you were sent here to do and to accomplish and the process of taking the Steps to Knowledge that will lead you towards the reconciliation.

God knows how difficult the world is. God is not running the world and every little event. But God is responding to great turning points in the history of humanity. God is aware of the great peril that exists for the human family as it faces a declining world and Intervention from races in the universe who are here to take advantage of human weakness and division.

Your purpose then is connected not only to your reconciliation, but also to the events of the world and the needs of humanity. Your role will be very specific, engaging with certain people for a certain purpose. You cannot ascertain this with the intellect, though you may try, and many have tried. It is something that will emerge on the horizon of your inner life once you are taking the Steps to Knowledge and are engaged in your preparation.

Your reconciliation is not simply to redeem you, but to provide a unique and important service to others and to the world itself. The Lord of the universes would not waste this opportunity to have your life be of value and meaning to others.

Regardless of what you have done to yourself previously, regardless of the degradation and the errors and the compromises you have made to your detriment, the power of this purpose can redeem you. You

THE POWER OF KNOWLEDGE

can be the lowest person on the Earth, and the power of Knowledge can still redeem you.

Every step you take towards Knowledge is a step towards your reconciliation—with your Source, with your Spiritual Family who have sent you into the world—a reconciliation with your deeper nature, a reconciliation with life. It is a reconciliation that emanates from Knowledge within you and calls forth that part of you that is identified with the world and is lost in the world.

What begins to bring you to the path of reconciliation is the realization that you really are lost in the world and that others around you have the same condition and the same liability. This realization, which is entirely honest and which is greatly needed, will disillusion you to the point where you realize you must seek a greater meaning for your life. This is the beginning of the reconciliation.

You may feel that you are not accountable to anything in particular, except perhaps your children and your direct family, your immediate family, but in reality you are accountable to those who sent you into the world. It is they who will be waiting for you when you leave this world. And before them, you will realize if you have achieved your objectives here or not.

Whatever the outcome, they will treat you with great love and deference, so there is no damnation, you see. God does not condemn Creation. But God has set into motion the forces of reconciliation that will redeem that small part of Creation that is living in Separation, that small part of Creation you call the physical universe. You cannot possibly fathom what this means or outpicture it for yourself. Of course not. This is beyond the reach of the intellect, as are most things of greater significance.

THE RECONCILIATION

Your task is to take the Steps to Knowledge and to have the honesty to realize that without this greater guidance within you, your decisions will be weak, predicated on weak assumptions, on shifting desires, on momentary attractions and, most importantly, based upon the grinding reality of fear that so pervades your life and other people's lives that it goes almost unnoticed except when it is expressing itself in extreme ways.

The constancy of this fear makes it disappear from people's awareness. They think it is just being normal—a normal kind of anxiety, a normal kind of inadequacy. When people express this, they say, "Well, that is just normal"—a normal state of fear and apprehension, a normal state of exhaustion and confusion. People have adapted to a miserable condition, and they call this normal.

But deeper down, at the level of your true nature, at the level of Knowledge, [this] is not really acceptable. When you come to realize this, it will be the turning point of your life, regardless of your age and circumstances, regardless of whether you are rich or poor, single or married, no matter what faith tradition you adhere to, or no faith tradition if that be the case. No matter what nation or culture or political persuasion of your government, it is all the same. It is the same whether you are human or whether you belong to another race in another world. It is the same dilemma, you see. It is not limited to the human condition. It is the condition of Separation itself.

Your mind will try to make Separation successful. It will try to be happy, wealthy and content and gather all the things and people it believes it must have to secure its happiness. But the more that it gathers, the more frightened it will be about losing the things that it has gathered. And the more apprehensive it will become as the years pass and you grow older and things begin to fade.

THE POWER OF KNOWLEDGE

People are striving at immense expense and cost to try to make Separation successful and enjoyable, fulfilling and complete, but they can never really quite do it, you see. It takes great humility to give up the pursuit, to finally realize that you need to be connected to a Greater Power—not the power of your government or the power of your community or the power of your religious affiliations or the power of your family or the power of anything in the world, but the Power of your Creator, a Greater Power. Even if you are not religious in your thinking and associations, it is all still the same. You will just describe it differently, that is all.

Life can serve you by disappointing you in this way, by bringing you to the true reckoning within yourself, which is the beginning of the reconciliation. If you realize you cannot really answer the bigger questions that will arise, then you must turn to a Greater Power, a Greater Source, however you define it. Though your definitions will be incomplete and perhaps even foolish at the outset, it is the beginning of a greater association.

God does not care what religion you belong to. God is not attached to the theology of any religion, for in the universe there are countless religions. God will respond to the turning of your life, to the opening of your heart, to the emerging need of the soul, the deepest need you have, which is the need to fulfill your purpose as the means of reconciliation.

Here service in the world is not a punishment. It is the process that allows Knowledge within you to emerge into your awareness and to become the most important force in your life. It is not [like] you are sent into the world to do penance, as if you were a convict that had to go out and do manual labor to fulfill your sentence. It is not like this

THE RECONCILIATION

at all. The service you render is what generates the reconciliation for you and what nourishes and fosters reconciliation for others.

For what is the most powerful evidence of God in the world but the evidence of selfless giving, the caring for others even if they do not care for you, the caring of the Earth even if the Earth seems indifferent to your existence? That is the most profound demonstration of the Creator there could be. This is what moves people. This is what opens people's hearts. This is what connects them to their deeper conscience and gives them a sense that they too have a greater connection and a greater responsibility in being in the world.

You cannot reconcile yourself. This is not an intellectual pursuit. You can formulate the most elegant belief system possible, but it is not the reconciliation. You are still lost in your thoughts. You are still disassociated from yourself. You are still disconnected. You are governed by beliefs and assumptions and have not really taken the greater journey yet.

This is a different kind of journey. You do not invent it. It is not the product of you patching together different religious or spiritual ideas that you find to be enhancing. It is not the product of having a grand philosophy or ideology. It is something more innate, more authentic, happening at a deeper level that is moving your life.

This is the beginning of the Great Attraction of the Creator for the Created. Once you begin to take the steps [towards] reconciliation, you will begin, very intermittently at first, to experience the Great Attraction. This is how God recalls you to your Source. It is from the Great Attraction.

THE POWER OF KNOWLEDGE

It is not by threatening you with Hell and damnation. It is not by promising you paradise, which you can only imagine as a physical place. It is not by winning you over by great promises of joy, ecstasy and fulfillment. Perhaps that is what is needed to persuade you at the level of your worldly mind, but deeper down, the Attraction is the Attraction.

It is the great Love operating within you, generating its own attraction. It is the great Love you will feel for certain people with whom you have a greater purpose and destiny, a Love that seems very different from the feverish, romantic pursuits that people give themselves to here.

The reconciliation is the most important thing. It is more important than anything else you create because this is what will reconcile you to your Source, and this is what will truly inspire others in being with you. To create useful things for society is valuable and has great merit, but even beyond this, there is your presence in the world and the power of what guides you and the meaning of what guides you.

This is what gives you extraordinary courage. This is what gives you extraordinary perseverance. This is what gives you the eyes to see and the clarity to discern what is true from what is untrue, what is good from what only looks good. This is how you tell the difference between a true association with another and a fleeting passion or desire.

God redeems the separated through Knowledge, in this world and in all worlds. It is fine that you cannot understand this intellectually or turn this into some kind of simple formula that you can believe in. Everything that God really does is incomprehensible, but that does not mean it cannot be experienced and appreciated.

THE RECONCILIATION

People who believe that God is managing every little thing in their life are underestimating the majesty and power of the Creator. For God is not managing every little thing in your life. It is your job to manage every little thing in your life. God is not saving the world. God has sent you here to save the world. You have a small but essential part to play. If you do not play this part, the world grows dark. Its prospects are diminished.

You cannot escape this responsibility and this accountability. It is part of what redeems you, gives you power and courage, but it is not a truth that you can negotiate with. No matter what the circumstances of your life, which will determine in part what you are able to do and accomplish here, the agreement and the commitment are still there.

The part of you that is connected to God cannot be ruled or utilized by the part of you that is still disassociated from God. That is why you cannot use Knowledge to get what you want. You can only follow Knowledge and allow it to bring you to a greater fulfillment and a greater reconciliation.

This is what you admire in truly creative and generous people. This is what you admire in those who demonstrate selfless giving, not only on a grand scale, but on a simple scale. This is the service that true parents provide for their child. This is the service a true citizen provides for their community.

This is the great motivating force. It may be confused with other selfish pursuits, and that is often the case, but once you remove that which is false, you see the power of reconciliation at work.

People want many things. They are afraid of losing what they have and not finding what they are seeking. People want many things. But

THE POWER OF KNOWLEDGE

deep down, beneath the surface of the mind, they are looking for the reconciliation.

This is what connects you with your life before this world and the life to come. This is what connects you and gives you integrity and ends the terrible conflict and confusion that people call a normal life. This is what brings peace to your deepest nature because finally it is being recognized and responded to. This is what will give you a different journey in life and bring into your life a quality of relationship you could not find otherwise. This is what will give you the eyes to see and the ears to hear. This is what will enable you to provide a greater service and a greater accountability.

Here you will have moments where you feel the Power and the Presence of Heaven, for just moments, for that is enough. Here you will be able to overcome your own fear and indolence. You will be able to overcome your weakness and your vulnerability because there is a greater power emerging within you, the power and presence of Knowledge.

You still have to be a functioning person in the world. You still have to take care of the innumerable tasks of being in the world, and many of these tasks will grow and become more important. This is not an escape from the world, but a preparation for the world, for engaging in the world in a greater way, with a greater incentive and a greater awareness.

God is calling the separated to respond—not to take them out of the world but to bring them into the world with a greater purpose, a greater direction and a greater power.

THE RECONCILIATION

You were sent here to serve, but you were also sent here to experience reconciliation. It is easy to feel reconciled when you are not here. [There] everything is obvious, everything is apparent. Your questions decline. Relationship is everywhere; it is omnipresent. You are understood. You understand.

But when you come into the world, you lose this. You are blind. You are ignorant. You are vulnerable. It is at this level that the reconciliation must occur. You cannot run home to Heaven or think that if you are a good boy or a good girl, you get to go to Heaven—whatever that looks like in your imagination. No, not at all. If you do well, you are given greater service. Beyond this world, you begin to serve those who remain behind. God is not going to waste your accomplishment, but employ it in greater ways.

Once you have gained the reconciliation, then you will naturally want to promote it and support it in others. This is the natural desire of the heart. You cannot keep reconciliation for yourself, as if you were holding some kind of wealth. It is something that must flow through you, and naturally it will.

God's New Revelation clarifies this, but it is present in all the world's great religions. But these truths have become obscured there, overlaid with belief, pageantry, history and misinterpretation. That is why the Revelation of God for this time and for the times to come must clarify these things in the simplest possible way and must repeat them constantly so that you can begin to understand and be reminded that you are here for a greater purpose, and that there is a greater reconciliation that must occur in your life and will occur as you begin to take the Steps to Knowledge and to respond to the deeper needs of your heart and your soul.

CHAPTER 8

WHO YOU ARE IS NOT YOUR MIND

As revealed to
Marshall Vian Summers
on October 29, 2009
in Boulder, Colorado

You are not your mind. You are not your intellect. Who you are is not your thoughts. You are not your beliefs. You are not your memories. You are not your conflicts. You are not those things that you identify with.

The mystery of who you are exists beyond the reach and the realm of the intellect and beyond the reality of the body. But you are inhabiting this body now. And the intellect is there to help you to navigate this world and to participate here. It is a marvelous vehicle of communication. It is exquisite, profound and capable of doing marvelous things if it is cultivated correctly. But for all students of Knowledge in all traditions, it is necessary to realize the difference between your real nature, your deeper nature, and the makeup of your mind and your system of beliefs, however organized or disorganized they might be.

That you live at the surface of the mind and do not know of its depths, its mystery and its true power and abilities—this must be a recognition, or you will think that spirituality is a belief or a system of beliefs. You will think that spiritual practice is about reinforcing ideas, reinforcing beliefs, and, of course, this is tremendously

95

THE POWER OF KNOWLEDGE

manipulated by government and religious institutions—the manipulation of belief because most people are not yet aware that who they are is not their minds, and so they think that what they think is what they are, and it represents their reality.

Once you are able to break this assumption and this fixation, a whole door begins to open to your inner life, where you will soon experience that you have a greater nature, a deeper nature beyond your thoughts and ideas. Sit still for twenty or thirty minutes, and this will become very apparent to you.

It is like the noise on the street—your surface mind—it is crashing and banging and moving and colliding. It is judging, it is comparing, it is fantasizing, it is remembering, it is projecting blame, it is projecting its will. It is doing all this. But if you were to step back from it, to close the doors, to close the windows and go into the inner sanctuary of your home, the sounds of the street would recede and eventually disappear completely.

It is like this in your mind. Once you sink below the surface of your mind, you will find there is a greater reality there that you know nothing about, a reality with many levels, and that you have deeper associations here and deeper relationships.

You have relationships with your Spiritual Family, who are not in the world. You have relationships with your Spiritual Family who are living in other worlds. You have a relationship with your Teachers, those Unseen Presences who watch over your development and who send you thoughts from time to time to assist you in opening yourself to the reality of your real life. And, of course, you have the power of Knowledge, the deeper Mind within you, the Mind that God created, not the mind that culture and the world created.

WHO YOU ARE IS NOT YOUR MIND

This deeper Mind is entirely different from your intellect and has great power and certainty. It is not governed by fear and desire. It is not driven by compulsion and anxiety. It does not need to assert itself and to defend itself and to overwhelm others to seek power and recognition in the world. It is only here to serve a greater purpose, which it alone is aware of within yourself.

Once you break your attachment to the surface of your mind and recognize that that is only a part that you play in the world—like a part an actor would play on a stage—then you can begin to see and feel and experience the deeper current of your life. This opens you in life to experience relationships that represent this deeper current, this deeper recognition, this greater purpose together.

This lessens the impact of fear. This lessens the impact of desire and compulsion. This breaks your fascination with your own fantasies. This breaks the chains of identification that keep you enslaved to a set of ideas and activities that have nothing to do with who you really are and why you are really in the world.

Anyone who has any spiritual depth, no matter what their tradition or period of history, has broken this fixation and identification with the surface of the mind. They know there are greater truths to be experienced that ideas alone cannot contain, that theories and philosophies and systems of thinking cannot fully represent.

They see the limits of science. They see the limits of the intellect. They see the limits of theology and philosophy. They recognize that there is a mystery to their lives and that they have the opportunity to experience this mystery and to express it to others. That is a great turning point, you see.

THE POWER OF KNOWLEDGE

But when you look out into the world, people are totally caught up. They cannot leave the street and seek the sanctuary within themselves. They are so caught up, always stimulating their mind—getting new thoughts, new beliefs and exercising their old beliefs and reinforcing their old beliefs and finding other people in relationship who can help them reinforce their beliefs. It is all an avoidance of fear—the emptiness, the fear of loss, the fear of not finding, the fear of losing, the fear of confusion, the fear of chaos, the fear of your own mortality, the fear of death and annihilation.

All this constant activity to reinforce one's identity is simply running away. It is running away from the reality that lives within you at this moment, which alone holds the greater purpose and meaning of your life. It is running away from yourself. It is running away from your own fear and uncertainty, constantly driven and caught up. It is not an accident this is happening. It is not merely circumstances.

People cannot sit still for five minutes. They cannot blame their circumstances for this. The time they spend in front of the mirror in the bathroom every day could be spent sitting quietly, practicing inner listening, opening up to the landscape of the mind and the great well of silence within oneself that brings peace and insight and power to the individual.

People are so caught up in their intellect, they cannot seem to find a way out of it, as if they are surrounded by barbed wire and they cannot find a way out. But sitting still and following your breath, or repeating a sound or a word, is enough if you stay with it, if you continue your practice and are not disappointed or frustrated that at first you find out just how much your mind is dominating you, and what a slave you are to your thinking and your beliefs and your memories and your fears and the projections of your fear.

WHO YOU ARE IS NOT YOUR MIND

Rich or poor, this is the bondage under which humanity struggles and suffers. Go to the richest places in the world and people are still slaves to the mind, slaves to their needs and their desires, their compulsions and their anxieties. Even if they are living in splendor, they act like servants—toiling away, unaware of what oppresses them, unable to see a way out.

Religion, then, becomes governed by the mind, by the intellect. It becomes a ritual, a belief, a social requirement, social validation. It loses its primacy, its intimacy, its fervency, its mystery and its grace.

Now you must go to the church or the mosque or the temple because you are expected to. And you are afraid of what might happen if you do not. And you ask God for things to help you, to save you, to give you what you want, to protect your loved ones.

Some requests are genuine and some are not. But do you seek an experience of union with the Divine? Do you seek to experience what lies beneath the surface of your mind? Do you seek to know your spiritual reality and nature, which exists beyond theological expectations and speculation?

You are totally caught up in the manifestation of life, but what about its mystery? Its purpose? Its meaning? These things can only be found beneath the surface.

You may create wonderful explanations, fantastic theories of belief, extraordinarily complex ideologies, but the mind cannot grasp the power of Spirit, or the reality or the wisdom of Spirit, which is the power and the wisdom of Knowledge within you. But to begin to engage in this deeper exploration and to build the skills, the patience and the determination you will need to proceed, you must begin to

THE POWER OF KNOWLEDGE

take the Steps to Knowledge—to learn how to focus your mind and to slip past its allurements and its fixations.

God has given you the purest spiritual practices you can find in practicing stillness and inner listening. And the practices are given in Steps to Knowledge. They do not require fantastic beliefs. They do not require idols of worship. They do not require heroic figures, saints and saviors and avatars. You can practice them in the next moment. You can practice them this evening or tomorrow morning.

You practice because you want to know the deeper reality of your life. And you know there is something there because you have always known there is something there. It is not a matter of belief.

Beliefs change. Beliefs are manipulated. Beliefs are reinforced, and then beliefs fall apart. The reason that people constantly have to reaffirm belief is that belief is inherently unstable because it does not have a deeper foundation. And until belief has a deeper foundation, it will be unstable and unreliable and can become very self-deceptive.

In meditation, you learn to step back from your mind and to find the calmness and the peace that allows your mind to open and your senses to become clear and sharp. Out of this comes a greater discernment and discretion in life.

You cease to talk so much and begin to listen more. You step away from constant stimulation so that you can stay with your own experience. You begin to value your experience more than your ideas, realizing your experience is far more true and far more reliable. You listen to others differently. You relate to others differently. You begin to experience the depth of nature as not merely scenery but as life force. You begin to experience the

WHO YOU ARE IS NOT YOUR MIND

mental environment of your life, the environment of thought and influence, and new worlds begin to open for you.

God cannot really do anything for you until you begin this path of liberation. You will not be liberated completely. That is not a realistic goal. But once you have begun to differentiate between your deeper experience and your intellect, then doors will begin to open for you.

Your life will begin to make sense. And you will begin to experience the deeper current of your life, which has always been flowing, in contrast to your plans and your goals and so much of how your life has been spent in the past.

Say to yourself: "I am not my mind. I am not my intellect." These are thoughts, too, but they give reference to a greater reality within you, which is not about thoughts. Here you do not denigrate the intellect, but you realize that it must be governed by a greater Spirit within you, and that your greater Spirit is governed by the Source of all spirituality.

Here the intellect is valued, so you want to cultivate it. You do not want to pollute it with ugly and violent things. You do not want to denigrate it with self-destructive, self-demeaning behavior. You want it to be clear and powerful. You want it to serve you rather than you serving it.

This is a great correction in your relationship with yourself, which is fundamentally your relationship with your mind and with your body. For you only have one Self, so your relationship with your Self is your relationship with the deeper reality within you. But from this reality, you have a relationship with your mind and your body, which must

THE POWER OF KNOWLEDGE

be wisely and compassionately governed and managed and directed, rather than left to direct themselves.

Your body is a wonderful vehicle. Without it, you could not communicate to people here. They could not hear you. They could not see you. They would not notice your presence, even if you were standing next to them. If you did not have a mind, you could not reach their mind. You would be invisible. They would not even know you were there. So the mind is a precious thing. The body is a precious thing, so mistreated in the world, so abused in the world, tragically.

But for you, you must find a way now to build a real relationship with your greater Self, your deeper nature, because this holds the key to your life and your future. And the closer you become to this, the more difficult it will be for you to make a mistake and to throw your life away.

Do not think that you are not throwing your life away, or that you are right where you need to be and that you are already guided and governed, for that is hardly the case. If you are honest with yourself, you will certainly have to admit this.

It is a great journey before you. And God has given you a way, a way to rediscover the power and the presence of Knowledge and its immense importance for your life and for your future. It is the most trustworthy thing there is.

As the world becomes more turbulent and chaotic in facing the Great Waves of change, you will need this strength and this guidance and this self-confidence. You will need to find this in others and support this in others, for it will be the strength of Knowledge and the

WHO YOU ARE IS NOT YOUR MIND

strength of genuine relationships that will protect you and guide you and lead you to your greater accomplishments in life.

The intellect does not know of these things. It can only speculate and hope and believe. But the certainty of your greater life is already held within you, like a secret cargo that you yourself cannot open. It must be called out of you, but to be called out of you, you must be ready. You must prepare. You must liberate yourself from the surface of your mind sufficiently that you can travel beneath it whenever it is necessary.

In this way, you become a medium between your Ancient Home and the world, between your physical reality and your spiritual reality. You become a vehicle for grace and power and contribution. This is your heart's desire. This is what you were created to do.

You were not created to live a miserable and chaotic life in a harsh and difficult world. That is not your true destiny. It may be your current reality, but it is not your true destiny. But ideas alone cannot assure you of this. You must experience it more deeply within yourself and in your true relationships with others.

Listen to these words. Listen to the Power and the Presence that is with these words. Hear them deeply. Do not dispute them. Do not use your mind as a kind of fence or barrier. Do not use your mind to hide. Do not use your mind to take issue with what is there to serve you most profoundly.

God has a plan for your life. You cannot figure it out with your intellect because it was not created by your intellect, and it far surpasses your intellect. That is why your religious beliefs can never

THE POWER OF KNOWLEDGE

be absolute unless you are foolish and arrogant. The Mystery will always exceed them and confuse them and liberate you from them.

Let this be your understanding.

CHAPTER 9

KNOWLEDGE AND THE LIMITS OF BELIEF

As revealed to
Marshall Vian Summers
on November 3, 2008
in Boulder, Colorado

You were born with two minds: an intellect that has been largely shaped by your culture, your family and your environment, and by your own judgments, assumptions and conclusions; but deeper down, there is a spiritual Mind, a Mind called Knowledge. It is called Knowledge because it is related to your ability to have profound insight and to access information that is beyond the reach of your five senses.

Knowledge is very unlike your surface mind. It does not judge. It does not speculate. It does not debate. It does not deal in the realm of ideas and possibilities, theories and principles. It is the seat of your power and integrity, and it holds for you your greater purpose for coming into the world, a greater purpose that you cannot access through your intellect.

The realm of belief is the realm of the surface mind, but Knowledge represents a deeper awareness and experience within yourself. This becomes all very confusing at the surface of your mind, for even if you did have a direct experience of Knowledge concerning something, you would surround it with your ideas, your

105

THE POWER OF KNOWLEDGE

assumptions, your conclusions and your attempt to associate it with other ideas and beliefs and so forth.

Many people have the unfortunate habit of trying to use all of their new experiences to affirm their old ideas. They try to use a profound and mysterious experience to somehow strengthen their ideas, their beliefs and even their prejudices. This is an unfortunate habit, and it must be broken at some point.

For Knowledge is occurring beyond the realm of your ideas and beliefs. That is what makes it powerful. That is what makes it reliable. It has not been conditioned by the world. It is not subject to seduction by the world or corruption in any form.

People, of course, have beliefs about Knowledge. Some people think it does not exist. Others think it does exist, but it only exists according to their notions and ideas, or perhaps the ideas of their religious practice or tradition.

At the level of ideas, you cannot know anything. You can only make assumptions and find agreement with others. Here it becomes very difficult to distinguish what you believe from what you really know. Aside from the obvious, like the sun coming up in the morning, and the winter returning at the end of the year, people do not know how to discern the reality of Knowledge within themselves from their own intellect and their own ideology or the ideology of others.

So when you think about Knowledge, you are using your ideas about Knowledge. But Knowledge is a profound experience. It transcends what your senses alone can report, and it most certainly transcends human logic or other systems of evaluation. So in that respect, it

KNOWLEDGE AND THE LIMITS OF BELIEF

remains mysterious. And yet it is the most natural experience you can have. It is just happening at a deeper level, that is all.

Here beliefs, particularly if they are well founded and if you identify with them too greatly, become a serious impediment to your ability to experience the power of Knowledge that God has placed within you. This Knowledge was given to you to guide you, to protect you from harm and to lead you to your greater fulfillment and a greater life in the world.

For many people of the world, Knowledge will not emerge because they live under such dreadful circumstances—under grinding poverty, or severe political oppression, or environments of immense insecurity where there is conflict and war. It is so unfortunate for the human family that this is the case because it denies the contribution that all of these people have been sent into the world to make. They are circumstantially oppressed, and their greater gifts in almost all cases will not emerge. Nor will they find the strength and the certainty that only Knowledge can provide.

But once you have met the basic requirements of life—you have a reliable source of food, water and shelter, and sufficient security in where you live, and some degree of a supportive network of relationships—then you can begin to entertain the deeper questions about your life. But these deeper questions can only be approximated by your intellect, and by the limits of belief.

You may believe, for example, that God is real, but the reality of God is primarily a profound experience. There are many people who may have a firm belief about God's existence, but have never had a profound experience of the reality of God or their connection with God, for that happens at a deeper level, at the level of Knowledge.

107

THE POWER OF KNOWLEDGE

One of the main areas of confusion here is that people believe that their mind is who they are. Never having a more profound and life-changing deeper experience of themselves, they think that their ideas and their intellect is who they are. Identifying, then, with the mind and the body, their whole identity becomes based upon their ideas, their beliefs and their doctrines.

This is extremely blinding, of course, and represents a fundamental error and confusion. It is the result of Separation from God, a Separation that has brought you into the world, to live in manifest reality and to face the harsh and demanding conditions of living in an environment that is constantly changing and that offers innumerable threats and uncertainties.

In truth, your intellect was established to be a vehicle of communication for Spirit, or Knowledge. And for this purpose, it is a magnificent instrument, a brilliant creation. But unless you realize that your true identity is beyond the intellect and beyond the formulation and the protection of your ideas, then you will be a slave to the intellect, and it will make a harsh and demanding ruler. It is oppressive in this regard, for while the intellect is a marvelous instrument of communication, and serves to evaluate the particulars of life with great skill and brilliance, it in truth makes a very poor God. It makes a very poor guide.

Fixed in its beliefs, constantly seeking approval and consensus with others, constantly afraid for its survival and fundamentally insecure without the presence of Knowledge to guide it, your surface mind is like an arrogant child. It is no longer serving in its true capacity. It is now assuming other roles, for which it has not been designed and within which it functions ineffectively and inefficiently.

108

KNOWLEDGE AND THE LIMITS OF BELIEF

Here minds conflict with other minds that have different ideas, that have different associations. Here people who identify with their culture or their group end up competing with those who identify with a different culture or group—competing for resources, competing for power, competing for ideological supremacy—when in fact, at a deeper level, they are all connected by Knowledge.

Here, at a deeper level, there is no conflict. For it all comes from the same Source. This is a part of you you did not create and the world did not create, the part of you that God created, the part of you that God has sent into the world to provide a unique contribution to a world in need.

This is not like the idea of a subconscious mind, which is like a storage area for information and past memories. No, no. Knowledge is the most alive part of you, the most dynamic part of you, the most creative part of you, and it is the only permanent part of you.

Since nearly everyone identifies with their ideas, thinking their ideas distinguish who they are and give them a place in society, Knowledge here becomes a kind of mystery. And if it is not disavowed completely, it is perceived with anxiety and apprehension.

At first, people try to use Knowledge as a kind of resource. They are going to try to use God and what God has created to fortify their beliefs, to give them greater acquisitions, power and influence in the world. But you cannot use Knowledge as a resource. It will not be used in this way, and in truth, it is far more powerful than your intellect. Here the mind is trying to use Spirit to get what the mind thinks it wants or needs.

THE POWER OF KNOWLEDGE

You can see here the problem, for the mind was meant to serve Knowledge, not the other way around. Belief is meant to serve Knowledge as an expedient, as a way of organizing one's thoughts and giving stability to one's perception and action. Even here belief is relative. It is only valued in terms of its usefulness in enabling the individual to function successfully in the world and to communicate successfully with others.

God is entirely beyond belief, and what God has placed within you to guide you is also beyond belief. You, of course, will have beliefs about it. You may have beliefs that reject it. You may have beliefs that accept it theoretically, but deny it in your own experience. You may say, yes, Knowledge exists, but only in this way, or only under these circumstances, or only within this doctrine or ideology. This, of course, represents the arrogance and the ignorance of the intellect.

Greater minds in the world and in the universe, of course, have seen the mind as a medium—the medium between your physical life in your body in the world and your spiritual life beyond the world. They see the intellect as a medium through which your five senses can report reality and your greater senses can report reality.

Knowledge is so important here because it can see through all deceptions. Perhaps you will experience this as what people call "a gut feeling," and people describe this in many different ways. But it is an experience of recognition about the truth or the falsity of something that defies intellectual evaluation and is not the product of intellectual evaluation. Some people call this experience intuition, but intuition as an idea is insufficient to enable you to comprehend the meaning, the power and the presence of Knowledge within your life.

110

KNOWLEDGE AND THE LIMITS OF BELIEF

For the student of Knowledge, who is learning to live under the guidance and direction of Knowledge, there is a kind of battle between their ideas and the reality of their true experience. Having previously based their identity upon their beliefs and the beliefs of others, they now find it very difficult to live without relying upon these beliefs. They feel, for brief periods of time, as if they do not know quite who they are. [Having] taken away the substitutes for Knowledge and yet not strong enough and connected enough to the experience of Knowledge, they feel temporarily lost.

This is the "wandering in the desert" phase of your greater education in Knowledge. Freed sufficiently from your reliance upon your own beliefs and recognizing the limits of belief, you are not quite sure who you are or what you are doing. And you have not progressed far enough up this mountain to see clearly the relationship between Knowledge and the mind.

So, for a time, you go through periods of great uncertainty. But this uncertainty is essential for your development because it is within this opening in your awareness that the power and the presence of Knowledge can arise within you. It is also here where you can begin to discern the power and presence of Knowledge in others, and see how distinct this is from belief and ideology.

When you look in the world, you see people fighting and killing each other over their ideas—their ideas of who they are, their ideas of what they think the truth is, their ideas about how governments should be run and, of course, their ideas about who and what God is, and what God wills for humanity. They are competing with and condemning each other and even generating warfare with each other over ideas. If they were guided by Knowledge, this would not be the case.

THE POWER OF KNOWLEDGE

Here it is very important to realize that if you are going to liberate yourself from your ideas, you must have a greater foundation within yourself emerging at the same time. It is dishonest to say that you do not really believe in anything because you really do believe in lots of things. Even to consider everything as being relative or dependent upon perspective is really a shadow system of beliefs, and when revealed it is shown to be nothing more than a defense mechanism. People here can be absolutely certain that there is no absolute certainty, but they are absolutely certain about that idea and other ideas that are associated with it.

So you can see here that the mind can fool itself. It can shift its allegiance between ideas, but it is still stuck in its own self-created reality. And the idea of creating a new or better reality in the mind only means you are moving from one cell to another. You are still inside the prison. You have not seen through the boundaries of the intellect, and you have not seen beyond the reach of your own emotions.

You are still living inside a box—a box of your own ideas, a box of other people's ideas, a box of your social, political and religious conditioning. And you do not live happily in this box or peacefully in this box because to base your identity upon ideas means that you are fundamentally insecure. And this also places you in opposition to others, who have very different ideas.

Here even your notions of establishing peace and harmony overlook the fact that you will have to deal with people who have very different ideas, and who do not want what you think you want, and who will oppose you in one way or another. Then what do you do about them? You negotiate, perhaps, but often without success.

KNOWLEDGE AND THE LIMITS OF BELIEF

The fundamental underlying problem here is that people are not recognizing one another at a deeper level. And they are not recognizing themselves at a deeper level. They are fixed in their ideas and their beliefs. They are entrenched in their positions—their political positions, their religious positions. And, rich or poor, people are living in a kind of servitude to a set of beliefs and assumptions and expectations that are oppressive to the human spirit.

Yet this does not mean that you are living, or meant to live, without form and structure, for society and civilization cannot function without form and structure. This does not mean you are going to live in the world without the intellect, without beliefs, because that is false and cannot be. Your beliefs give your mind structure and enable it to function with consistency and in conjunction with others in the world.

The difference really is where you stand with your own ideas and the degree to which you are connected to the deeper current of your life. Here you realize that Knowledge is really the power and the presence and is the essence of who people are. You look for Knowledge in others, and you look to see with whom you can have a deeper connection and a more serious conversation and engagement. Instead of struggling over ideas and beliefs and principles, you look for a deeper connection. This tends to moderate your ideas and your association with your ideas. For, after all, ideas are only ideas; they are phantoms in the mind.

There are practical ideas that are essential to make civilization work, to create technology, to provide a sustainable environment, a habitable environment for people. But that is not where the conflicts really arise. Conflicts arise more around ideas with which people identify themselves. They think they are a Christian or a Buddhist or

THE POWER OF KNOWLEDGE

an American or a Brazilian or a Chinese. They think that is who they are, but that is not who they are. Who they are is beyond definition. It is even beyond distinction at the level of ideas.

When that door is open within yourself, it tempers extremism and eccentricity. It tempers condemnation of others. It gives you a deeper perspective, and makes you more cautious about condemning others or dismissing others because they do not hold to your views or your ideas.

At a deeper level, there is recognition and respect because you experience another's humanity, and you recognize that everyone is struggling to survive in the world, and to varying degrees everyone is trying to come to terms with the reality that they really are not of the world. They have a deeper spiritual nature and a deeper Intelligence called Knowledge.

Many people deny this altogether. Other people try to find some kind of way of allowing this reality to be in their minds, at least at the level of an idea. And other people are having a profound experience of Knowledge. It is altering their views, and it is changing their relationship with their mind.

You see, you have a relationship with your mind and with your ideas. But this means that who you are is not your mind or your ideas because a relationship requires at least two. You may say to yourself: "Well, my ideas are a part of me." Well, they are certainly part of your experience of yourself and may even dominate your experience of yourself and close the door upon having any deeper experience of yourself. But the fact that you can watch your mind and that you can direct your mind means that who you are is not your mind.

KNOWLEDGE AND THE LIMITS OF BELIEF

There is a relationship, yes, but you are dealing with different realities now. You can even learn to still your mind. And in the study of Steps to Knowledge, which is God's Gift of preparation to the world, you can learn to still your mind and enter the well of silence beneath the surface of your mind—a wonderfully refreshing and peaceful environment and an environment that takes you deeper to the experience of Knowledge within yourself.

This deeper journey, which represents life's greatest accomplishment, is where your spiritual nature becomes really evident. It is beyond the limits of doctrines and beliefs. You may create beliefs about it, you may try to fit it into an existing doctrine, but the experience itself defies definition.

This changes your relationship with your mind and shows you you have a relationship with your mind, and you are not really to merely be a slave to your ideas or the ideas of others. This invites you to live life at a deeper level, to experience the real purpose and direction of your life, which all becomes revealed as you go deeper within your own mind.

There are deeper currents within you that are not altered by the events of the day or the opinions of others or your emotional states or your immediate circumstances. This is where you find true direction. This is where God influences your life. And depending upon your relationship with your mind and the kind of ideas that you hold to, this deeper current can express itself into your outer life. This represents real progress.

Therefore, you must realize that your ideas are not absolute. They are only positions that you take. Some of these positions are extremely

115

THE POWER OF KNOWLEDGE

blinding and lead you to condemn others and lead you into conflict with others. In that, they represent real impediments.

Some people believe their religion is the only religion, and that everyone else is going to be condemned to Hell. You can see that they think their ideas are defining reality, or that their ideas were given them by God and represent absolute truth, in which there is no variance. This leads them to condemn others, to fight others and to become isolated in the world. Here they are slaves to their beliefs. They will even die for their beliefs. They will kill others for their beliefs. Or they will create mayhem for their beliefs.

This is the result of identifying with your mind, thinking that who you are is your mind and your body, and that your thoughts define you. This is the reality of Separation, where people are self-defined and live by those definitions and can see nothing beyond those definitions. They are blind, and they are destructive in the world—divisive, contentious, self-righteous, afraid to consider anything else. They are so identified with their thoughts that they must constantly reaffirm their thoughts, reaffirm their faith and reaffirm their beliefs.

Because ideas are unstable, they are not absolute truth. Even your interpretation of the sacred texts is an interpretation. You can see here how people would feel insecure when they realize that their ideas are only approximations, only attempts at comprehension. Where then is the basis of their lives? Where is their real foundation? What gives them real stability and certainty and a sense of continuity in life?

This certainty, this foundation, this continuity must come at a deeper level. If it is ideas only, or the slavish adherence to beliefs and

KNOWLEDGE AND THE LIMITS OF BELIEF

doctrines, then you are really are not seeing or knowing anything. You are a complete slave to a set of ideas alone.

Here you do not see that God is speaking to everybody—even those who do not believe what you believe, even those who do not adhere to your religion, those of other countries and tribes and groups who might live very differently from you and have different social customs and values. God is speaking to them.

God does not only speak to the people of one faith tradition, as if they were the chosen people, as if they were God's favorite, because God does not function at the level of ideas. God is not a super intellect because God exists beyond the physical reality. And beyond the physical reality you do not need ideas in the way that you think of them now. Ideas are related to form, to people, places and things and to the interpretation of events, which are people, places and things. God lives beyond this reality.

That is why the idea of a Judgment Day at the end of life is so ridiculous. Why would God condemn you when God knows what you are going to do and why you are going to do it? That is why God has put Knowledge within you to guide you, to protect you and to lead you to a greater life, to experience this great endowment. This is God's Gift to you.

You must go beyond belief. You must open yourself to have profound experiences within yourself. Instead of following your thoughts, you must learn to still your mind so you can feel the deeper reality that exists below the surface.

When you become strong with Knowledge and Knowledge can shine through you more greatly, you will look at other people and they will

THE POWER OF KNOWLEDGE

seem like they are living in chains. Rich or poor, they are living with a yoke, like oxen pulling a wagon, the wagon of their beliefs. You will begin to see what real liberation means, and where the power of liberation comes from, and how it is available to people of all faith traditions and people without a faith tradition, people from all nations, lands and cultures.

God does not discriminate. God knows that not everyone can follow one teacher, one teaching or one tradition. God does not function at the level of doctrines and beliefs.

This then requires that you open yourself to the mystery and the power of your life, and that you cannot create the way and the path. This is not the result of an eclectic approach, where you choose what you like from this tradition or that teaching, for that is all preference in the mind, and it is the mind you need to get beyond.

You need to poke your head above the surface of the earth. If you are living underground in your intellect all the time, you will not know anything, you will not see anything, and you will try to use all of your experiences to shore up and to affirm your belief, thinking that that is your identity.

When you reject the reality of God's Presence in your life, which is Knowledge, you reject it based upon ideas and upon tradition, which is the history of ideas and beliefs. Here ideas and beliefs become the reason you cannot forgive, the reason you cannot recognize another, the reason you cannot be compassionate, the reason that you will go to war, the reason that you will condemn others, the reason you will live a life of anger and frustration, the reason you cannot know yourself, the reason you cannot experience the Grace and the Power of God.

118

KNOWLEDGE AND THE LIMITS OF BELIEF

When you deny this deeper reality and your Source, you have only one place you can go, and that is your ideas. If you cannot find your true foundation, your true certainty, your true power in Knowledge that God has placed there, then you must seek it elsewhere, and the only place you can do this is in your ideas. It is the problem fundamentally of Separation.

Without God, you are insecure and unstable and have no assurances. And you face a life of grave uncertainty, a life with so many challenges, a life that is filled with so many dangers to your existence and to your well-being.

You really only have two choices here: you have Knowledge and you have belief. Knowledge will use belief and guide belief, but belief without Knowledge is blind and is alone and will only seek out others who have similar beliefs. It is the problem of Separation.

Who you are is not your mind and your body, but a greater Spirit inhabiting the mind and the body, and using the mind and the body as vehicles of communication in the world. Yes, the body is important. It must be maintained in a high degree of health. Yes, the mind is important. It must be cultivated and developed to be a successful vehicle of communication. It will have ideas, beliefs and assumptions, but these must always be flexible to meet the reality and the conditions of life.

Here instead of thinking your beliefs are the final arbiter of truth and are absolute, you see that they are all theories, subject then to a greater revelation. Not fixed, not defensive, they are all theories because they are all theories.

THE POWER OF KNOWLEDGE

The deeper recognition happens beyond the realm of the intellect. You may create ideas and evaluations of these experiences to your benefit, perhaps, but the experience itself is happening at a deeper level. It is getting to this deeper level that represents the focus of religion and spiritual practice in all of its forms.

Then the question is: Can you experience Knowledge in another? Does another have a deeper connection, or are they just living out their ideas and beliefs, identifying with their thoughts and with the traditions of thought?

People find security in traditions of thought, but if they cannot experience their own real nature, if they cannot experience the deeper current of their life, then their thoughts, no matter how great the tradition surrounding those thoughts, are really depriving them of the greater foundation and certainty that God has provided.

Here being a Christian, or a Muslim, or a Jew, a Hindu, or any [religion], is a pathway that best suits you to experience the deeper current of your life. Many people will pursue this outside of these great traditions. For all the great religious traditions were fundamentally initiated by God to reunite the mind with the Spirit, and to bring the mind under the direction of the Spirit. Here the mind is like the steward of the soul until the king can return or the queen can return, the true ruler of life can return.

People think that Knowledge is just a kind of greater intelligence, a greater intellect, but Knowledge does not function like your surface mind. Knowledge within you is connected to Knowledge within everyone, so there is no "your Knowledge" and "my Knowledge." People may argue over their interpretations of their experiences, or

KNOWLEDGE AND THE LIMITS OF BELIEF

their interpretations of life, but at the level of Knowledge, the debate and the war of words and ideas becomes increasingly irrelevant.

That is why Knowledge is the great peacemaker in the world. And that is why Knowledge will bring power, certainty and insight into your life, to teach you how to use your mind, how to use it as the marvelous vehicle of communication that it is, and how to take care of your body without identifying with it. It will teach you how to be an immortal Being living in a temporary world—to serve that world, to connect deeply with others, and to fulfill your mission for coming into the world, which will be your greatest satisfaction and will meet the deepest need of your soul.

Let this be your understanding.

CHAPTER 10

THE GREATER INTELLIGENCE

As revealed to
Marshall Vian Summers
on September 4, 2015
in Boulder, Colorado

Certainly, people have a notion of intelligence. How clever or capable a person's mind may be in certain situations, how well educated a person may be along certain lines of work or employment, how clever one might be and artistic one might be—all these things are considered markers of intelligence. But they only bespeak one aspect of intelligence within you.

The intellect and its development, or lack of development, is what people usually regard as intelligence. But there are different kinds of intelligence, and the greatest Intelligence within you remains hidden beneath the intellect, beneath the surface of the mind. It is as if the intellect were the visible part of the iceberg, and below the water line, the main body of the iceberg exists out of sight.

It is so much like your mind, you see. The intellect is at the surface—conditioned by the world, educated by the world, blinded by the world, fooled by the world, enraptured with the world, terrified of the world.

It is like the turbulent surface of the seas, whipped every which way by the winds of the world, without any seeming direction or purpose. But like the ocean itself, deep beneath the surface, the great currents of the

THE POWER OF KNOWLEDGE

world are moving the world's waters—relentlessly, purposefully—governed now by greater forces, even celestial forces.

And so it is with you. You live at the surface of your mind. You are dominated by your intellect and your ideas. You may even believe you are your ideas, or they represent who you are, and who you are in society, who you are to yourself perhaps, even perhaps—if you are religious—who you are to God. This is defined by your religious beliefs and affiliations. But this is only a small part of intelligence.

What the world will need increasingly in the future in the face of the Great Waves of change and in the face of Intervention from races from the universe who are here to take advantage of your weakness and divisions is intelligence, at every level of intelligence. It is the one resource that humanity seems to be lacking collectively.

While people may be brilliant within a narrow band of application, broadly speaking, very few people have wisdom and capability.

This will make it more difficult for you to adapt to a changing world, to a heating world, to a world of cataclysmic climate change and resource depletion, and competition and conflict.

People will feel helpless and hopeless in the face of these things because they have never brought their intelligence to bear upon these kinds of forces that have plagued humanity throughout history, to a certain degree.

But now you are facing change on a level never seen in the world before—change in your environment, change in your climate, change in your circumstances on a level never seen by all of humanity before.

THE GREATER INTELLIGENCE

But people are unaware. They are unprepared. They are maladapted. They are unintelligent when it comes to these greater things. They have never given it much attention. They think it is someone else's problems, or that someone else will fix things for them, at some level, in some way, though they have no idea how. This is an unintelligent response to real life situations.

The richer people are, the more incapable they can become in this regard, the more fixated they are on their possessions and their goals, their hobbies, their fantasies, their predicaments. They do not look over the horizon to see what is coming. They do not assess the situation on a regular basis to see if their foundation is sound and secure.

The poor people are living at the edge of nature, vulnerable at every turn. While their situation is far more tragic, often they are far more capable of understanding what is going on around them. And though they do not have the power or the wealth to prepare or to position themselves more favorably in the face of these things, there could be greater Intelligence here.

The farmer knows the ways and the winds of the world. The sailor knows the waves and the winds of the world. Anyone who must survive in nature has a greater scope and is observing things around them at all times, just as the animals do, the intelligent animals.

But people are living in their own little personal reality. They are living in a dream or a nightmare of that reality.

Knowledge within them, the greater Intelligence, will give them signs, but they will not heed it or hear it, or [they will] think it is something else.

THE POWER OF KNOWLEDGE

What humanity will need in the future is Intelligence, but not just intellectual intelligence. It will need the greater Intelligence that God has put within each person to guide them, to prepare them, to protect them and to lead them to a greater life of service and meaning in the world, even under the radically changing circumstances of life.

For you have been sent into the world to be in these circumstances, and Knowledge within you knows exactly what this means. It is not governed by the world. It is not afraid of the world. It is not governed by your attitudes and your beliefs, your condemnation of others, or your issues with life or God, whatever they may be.

God has given you the real Intelligence. It is not the only intelligence within you, for your worldly wisdom is very important, to whatever extent it has been developed and cultivated.

The more you can become educated intellectually, recognizing the realities of the world rather than merely human ideas about it, the more Knowledge can move through you and direct you correctly.

But be very clear that intellectual brilliance does not represent the power of Knowledge. People can be brilliant, but utterly blind in the rest of their lives and affairs—be as foolish as anyone, make the most ridiculous decisions, be convinced by the most unconvincing persuasions. Though they may be brilliant in one area, even if they are celebrated as being brilliant, the rest of their life can be a complete mess.

So be very clear that We are talking about Intelligence now at a greater level—within you and within everyone, waiting to be discovered. This Intelligence must guide the intellect, or the intellect

THE GREATER INTELLIGENCE

will continue to be dominated by its reactions to the world, by its ideas and fixations. When that is the case, you cannot see; you cannot know; and you cannot respond when Heaven is giving you wisdom and signs to hold you back, to keep you from moving in a direction that does not represent your destiny.

For you do have a destiny because you were sent here for a greater purpose. But if that purpose is not being realized, if you are not moving in that direction, if you are stranded somewhere in a set of circumstances that does not represent this destiny, then you will feel a restlessness and a frustration where nothing can relieve you until you come to your deeper senses and begin to take stock of your life, and to ask yourself, "Am I living the life I was truly meant to live?"

That is an intelligent question, but it does not have an easy answer, for the answer is not an idea. The answer is a pathway to follow. Mysterious it is. It is beyond the realm of your intellect, so you cannot fully understand it. But it will feel very natural to you, and very real. And the further that you will respond to this, the more you will feel right about your life and have a sense that there is a real purpose there—not of your invention, not a purpose that someone else has invented for you, but a real purpose that God has put there.

It is not a definition. People will say, "Well, just tell me what it is!" But it must be revealed to you step by step. You must prove your ability to respond to it and to follow it and to be worthy of it.

Great gifts, great messages, great realizations never come all at once if they come from a true source.

THE POWER OF KNOWLEDGE

The way out of your dilemma will not be your invention. The way out of this jungle of your mind and circumstances will not be something you invent or someone else invents for you.

For only God knows the way out of this. For only God knows what you are really here to do, whom you must meet, what you must accomplish, what you must avoid.

This is not to place you in a monastery or a convent. It is to put you out into the world, with the Power of Heaven to be your rudder, to keep you on track.

Your mind, your intellect, so proud it may be of its ideas and accomplishments, will have now to submit to a greater power within you.

Yet the greater Intelligence needs the lesser intelligence to be most effective in the world. So what you have learned; what you have accomplished; the wisdom you have developed; the clarity and certainty you have accomplished, to whatever degree, are all important. It makes your vehicle more competent. It makes your mind sharper. It makes you able to face challenge and difficulty and live with questions you cannot yet answer.

Here you do not disappear into God. You begin to regain your true relationship with God. And you become a person who was sent into the world to do something important and significant, however humble it may be and seem. It will be your greatest joy to do this.

Where you have been unsuccessful in finding true happiness in other things—other pursuits, other relationships, in romance, in the

THE GREATER INTELLIGENCE

pursuit of wealth, or adventure—nothing but your true purpose and destiny can satisfy the deeper need of your soul.

Once you come to experience this, then you have reached a real turning point in your life. And you will begin to turn to the greater power that can move you from within, and hold you back from within.

Now you have the greater Intelligence of Knowledge, which represents the part of you that is still connected to God. Now you have your intellect to be developed in a more appropriate and constructive manner. Now you have skills to develop.

Now you have the Four Pillars of your life to build: the Pillar of Relationships, the Pillar of Work and Providership, the Pillar of Mental and Physical Health and the Pillar of Spiritual Development and Awareness. Like the four legs of a table, they must all be built, you see. And your table will only be as strong, your foundation will only be as strong, as the weakest of these Pillars. Much of your foundation work in learning and living The Way of Knowledge that God's New Message for the world presents will be building this foundation.

For you must be in the right place with the right people for the right purpose, or Knowledge cannot give you a greater pathway to follow. Your greater work cannot be revealed to you because you are not in a position to recognize it or to bring it into existence.

Knowledge knows where you have to go. You must learn to follow. But as you follow, you will have to use your mind carefully to discern other people, to discern your environment, for there are many hazards along the way.

THE POWER OF KNOWLEDGE

Here you do not abandon the intellect for some kind of grand spiritual experience. Instead, your intellect is brought into greater service and is given a greater requirement for development and constructive education.

What do We mean by this? We mean that your intellect must learn about the Great Waves of change that are coming to the world, to face this with as much courage as you can, as objectively as you can.

You must learn about the condition of your community and your nation, and to a greater extent, the communities of the world.

You must learn about humanity's exposure and vulnerability to a universe full of intelligent life, which is revealed for the first time through God's New Revelation for the world.

You must learn about the Greater Community of life in this part of the universe, which is being revealed for the first time through God's Revelation for humanity.

There is much to be learned. There is much to be unlearned. There is much to be reconsidered and changed. There is a lot of work to do at the level of your mind. It is full of memory and grievances and persuasions that weaken you and that trouble you, even haunt you.

That is why people cannot sit still for five minutes—running all the time, chasing after everything and anything, being stimulated every moment so they will not feel their true condition. They will not come to their deeper senses.

You cannot go into the future with a mind like that, or you will not survive. You will not succeed. You will not be safe. You will not know

130

THE GREATER INTELLIGENCE

what to do, and you will follow others who do not know what to do. You will be terrified, frustrated and angry, turning against others. It is a prescription for disaster at a level never seen here before. That is why this Calling is so urgent, you see. That is why God has given a New Message for humanity at this critical turning point.

Already, the Great Waves of change are striking all over the world. Already, there is an Intervention underway from races who are here to take advantage of you, posing as being benign and spiritually advanced, when in fact they are nothing more than resource explorers, who are clever and who know how to persuade people.

These are the greater dilemmas that are coming over the horizon that most people are unaware of. And not only are they unaware, they do not want to become aware because they do not have the strength to face it. It would shatter their dreams. It would upset their plans. All of a sudden, all their ideas upon which they have built their understanding will be greatly threatened and upset. How many people in history have fallen with these same assumptions, same problems, same lack of intelligence?

This [greater] Intelligence is not fearful, but it is observant. It does not condemn others, but it does recognize errors, problems and risks. This Intelligence is not hopeless because it is born of Knowledge within you.

Your mind can go from hope to hopelessness in a moment—so fragile is your certainty, so thin your layer of confidence, so easily destroyed and upset are your assumptions.

It is to take you out of this pathetic and vulnerable state that God is calling to you now through the New Revelation, to build and to

131

THE POWER OF KNOWLEDGE

receive a greater Intelligence that is your inheritance here on Earth. In fact, it represents your purpose here on Earth.

For without this, you will not be able to navigate the difficult times to come. You will be helpless and hopeless. Or you will believe in some great solution. Or you will assume that technology will take care of it. Or the government will take care of it. Or some alien force will take care of it. So foolish this is, so unintelligent, so weak, so vulnerable.

The Calling is for you to become strong and competent. It is not about looking good. It is not about perfection. It is not about enlightenment or glory or bliss. It is about surviving in a difficult world and becoming a force for good there, a force of contribution.

For God knows what is coming to the world. And through the Revelation, God is trying to prepare you, to warn you, to bless you, to give you the pathway to build real strength, certainty and competence while others around you continue to be foolish and live in denial.

You must use all aspects of your intelligence, not just one. You must use your intellect. You must use your physical capabilities. You must use your natural responses to the world, to a certain degree. You must use your education. You must use your mistakes and your disappointments to help prepare you, for wisdom is born of these things. But most importantly, you must gain access to the greater Intelligence that lives within you, waiting to be discovered.

You must know the entire iceberg, not only the tip that rests above the water line. Then you become complete. Then you really become who you are. Before that, there is no hope of you understanding who

THE GREATER INTELLIGENCE

you are. It is just a nametag, or an identity, or a definition. There is nothing real or substantive about it at all.

But here you are engaging with all of your intelligence. And because Knowledge's purpose is wholly compassionate and productive, it will not give you the power to become a tyrant, or to dominate others, or to use everyone and everything to build wealth or luxury for yourself. For Knowledge has no interest in these things.

The mind cannot use Knowledge for its purposes. But Knowledge must use the mind for its purposes. That is the true hierarchy of power within you. And that is the true relationship between your mind, your heart and your soul.

Look around you at people and see what they are doing. See what they are reading. See what they are concerned with. See what distracts them. And ask yourself: Is this intelligent? Not whether it is good or bad. Is it intelligent? Are they functioning in an intelligent manner? Are they recognizing the circumstances of their life truly? Are they preparing for the future? For all intelligent life must live in the moment and prepare for the future, not one without the other.

Are they becoming weaker or stronger? Are they becoming more capable or less capable? Are they investing themselves in things that have real substance and destiny, or are they merely wasting their time, their youth and their resources?

Bring these same questions to bear on your life and your past, and you will see you have lived without Knowledge. You have all the evidence you need of what this was like—how unfulfilling it was, how little substance it really gave you, how really [little] benefit it gave you, how unfulfilling it was in the end.

133

THE POWER OF KNOWLEDGE

This is the challenge of receiving a New Message from God. It is not about bliss. It is not about enlightenment. It is not about getting into Heaven or avoiding going to Hell. This is not the time to be concerned with such things. You do not even know what these things really mean. It is time to prepare, to do a deep evaluation of your life, to ask yourself the most fundamental questions.

Knowledge within you will help you in this regard if you approach this sincerely, with determination. You will feel what is right and what is not right. You will feel what has inspiration and what does not have inspiration. You will feel what has purpose for your life and future and what does not.

It is only by living with real questions that the deeper answers can come to you, deeply from within you. And they will be the signs that there is a greater Intelligence living there—watching you, watching your life. It has always been there—watching you, watching your life, watching your mistakes, watching your indulgences, watching how you have harmed yourself and others in subtle and obvious ways.

You need not fear God's punishment, for God has given you the blessing, the warning and the preparation. God's intention is to save humanity from its current trajectory and path, which will only lead to destruction of life in this world.

Be intelligent. Build Intelligence. Exercise Intelligence and it will grow. Your intellect will become stronger, more certain. Your energy will grow because it is not being wasted on people, places and things that have no meaning and value. Your body will become stronger because you will take care of it now, realizing its importance as your vehicle in this world. Your emotions will become clearer as they are

THE GREATER INTELLIGENCE

truly directed. You will see a way out of the impasse of your life. For there is a door waiting for you, and it has already been opened.

CHAPTER 11

THE BRIDGE

As revealed to
Marshall Vian Summers
on November 9, 2013
in Boulder, Colorado

You were born with two minds: the deeper Mind that God has given you, the Mind you had before you came into the world, the Mind you will have once you leave the world; and you have a worldly mind, shaped and conditioned by your experience of the world and by your response to all those experiences and all the influences that have shaped your thinking, attitudes and beliefs since the day you were born.

The deeper Mind within you is with you today. It is still connected to God. It is still part of Creation. It is wise and fearless and uncorrupted by the world. But you do not live in this Mind, not yet, for it is greater Knowledge within you.

You live in your worldly mind, with all of its turbulence, its desires, its fears, its distractions, its obsessions, its unresolved conflicts and grievances and so forth. In your worldly mind, you seek comfort and reprieve from all these things, but there is little comfort there to be found. For your worldly mind is not built on who you really are and why you came into the world and who sent you here and for what purpose.

It is building the bridge between these two minds that is of greatest importance now. For you cannot understand your real nature, your

THE POWER OF KNOWLEDGE

purpose, your destiny living in your worldly mind. You can only have beliefs and assumptions regarding this. They are certainly weak and inadequate and so often completely false that you cannot rely upon them for anything.

You seek relief from the tribulations of the world and the conflicts of your life, but real resolution lives deeper within you—beyond the surface of the mind, beyond the reach of the intellect, beyond belief, beyond conjecture.

It is this bridge you must build, and that is why God has provided the Steps to Knowledge—to bring your worldly mind into alignment and service to the deeper Mind within you. For this is its true function, and here the [worldly] mind can become a beautiful thing, a magnificent instrument of communication, a magnificent instrument to solve problems of a practical nature.

Without this deeper Knowledge to guide you and the Power of Creation to guide you, your worldly mind becomes a prison, a fortress, a place from which you cannot escape, a thing that haunts you and binds you and encloses you and takes you away from reality—within yourself and within the world.

If you can sit quietly and begin to observe yourself, you will see how dominated you are by this worldly mind and how chaotic it really is. Though you establish patterns of thinking and behavior; though you have the routines that you follow, you are profoundly unaware of who you are, where you are going and why you are here.

For these questions can only be answered at a deeper level, at the level of Knowledge. But Knowledge will not merely provide answers.

THE BRIDGE

It will take you to the life you were meant to live, which you are not really living now, not yet.

People exhaust the intellect trying to understand greater things, trying to piece together a sense of reality on a larger scale, trying to understand their own inclinations and conflicts and contradictions. But at the level of Knowledge, these things become clear, evident and in some cases even unimportant. For Knowledge knows who you are and why you are here, who you are seeking to meet and what you must accomplish. It knows your real gifts and where they must be given, things the intellect could never ascertain.

Here you must learn to listen more deeply within yourself and to stop complaining about the world so that you can begin to see and to listen and to learn how to be still so that you can feel the nature of your deeper experience, which emanates from the level of Knowledge.

Without this bridge, you cannot respond to Knowledge adequately. It is speaking to you every day, but you will not hear it, for your mind is dominated by other things—by overactivity, by distractions and problems, by desires and fantasies. Knowledge is with you, but you are somewhere else. It is only when you come to realize your real condition here and how much suffering and confusion it is creating for you that you will seek to gain a greater certainty.

Here Heaven can really help you. Before that, you were adrift and lost and unwilling to respond. You were trying to create your own reality. You were trying to make Separation work, the Separation that has brought you into this world, with your plans, your schemes and your goals leading to confusion, uncertainty and depression.

THE POWER OF KNOWLEDGE

For you cannot make Separation work, try as you may. Everyone around you is trying so desperately to find happiness somewhere and to protect whatever they have that they think will give them comfort and security. It is really a desperate situation from which there seems to be no escape or relief.

This will become clear to you as you become honest with yourself, as you are able to reflect upon your real condition and what dominates your mind and awareness, as you come to recognize your compulsions and obsessions and inability to respond to things of a greater nature and meaning.

This creates a crisis internally because your soul requires that you respond to Knowledge and that you learn to follow Knowledge and allow Knowledge to prepare your life and reshape your life for a greater experience in the world.

This is the revolution internally, the most important revolution there can be anywhere, at any level of existence. It occurs gradually, through many steps and stages, many turning points, where you will have to choose again to continue as the power and emphasis within you shifts from your obsessive intellect to a deeper, more quiet power within you.

God does not punish evil because God knows that without Knowledge, evil will arise. God will not send anyone into Hell and damnation because God knows without Knowledge, people will be in error and will make grievous mistakes, even criminal acts, for they are governed by fear and anger and not the grace of Knowledge.

That is why God and God's New Revelation for the world have provided the bridge. For without this, what is religion but high ideals,

THE BRIDGE

strict observances, admonitions, restraints and cruel punishment if you should fail, which of course you will, eventually?

Without the bridge, the greater life is unattainable. The poets may sing of it. The great teachers may speak of it. The great Messengers may demonstrate it. But for everyone else, it is essentially unattainable because they do not have the bridge.

You cannot go into an inspired, sacred life living in your worldly mind. Oh, yes, it will attempt to build temples and chapels and mosques. It will parade as a spiritual person, reciting the scriptures and admonishing those who do not agree.

But you are still lost on the shore. You cannot enter the deeper water. You are pacing the beach, trying to understand, but you cannot yet enter the deeper water. You cannot even get your feet wet. You think on your own, living in Separation, you can understand your greater nature and purpose in the world and why God has sent you here and what you must do and whom you must meet, what you must refrain from and what you must build and emphasize?

The scriptures cannot teach you this, for it is wisdom that must come from Knowledge within you. The scriptures can only create guidelines and generalities that can be easily misapplied and misunderstood. Despite their wisdom and importance, people misuse these all the time.

When you realize your life is adrift, that you are living upon assumptions that have little basis in reality and that your mind is governed by fear—the fear of loss, the fear of not having, the fear of being unfulfilled, the fear of poverty, the fear of rejection, the fear of illness and calamity, the fear of death, adrift, living in Separation, in a

THE POWER OF KNOWLEDGE

world that is unpredictable and growing more dangerous and complicated every day, this will be your core experience no matter what frivolity you try to establish above and beyond it or how many distractions you keep for yourself. Even the attempt to work endlessly becomes a kind of avoidance and obsession because you cannot face or will not face your core experience.

That is why it is at times of great disappointment, loss or bereavement that people really come to a deeper place of reckoning within themselves, for it is in these experiences that the allurements of the world have no value. You are not even tempted. They are meaningless and pointless. They are charades. There is nothing of substance there.

It is in these times that most people finally come to ask the real questions. If they ask these questions with great sincerity and determination, Heaven will respond. Then Knowledge within them will have the opportunity to reach their awareness and to speak to their honest appeal.

This is the beginning, but there still must be the bridge because you have to move from your former life and state of mind into a new kind of life and state of mind. That does not happen overnight. That does not happen with a flash of a revelation alone. That does not happen even in a moment of great self-honesty and sobriety.

It is not based upon an insight. It is not based upon one moment of prescience or self-awareness. It is a journey you must take. It is the bridge, the long bridge. You must walk this bridge because there is so much for you to unlearn and to correct within yourself.

THE BRIDGE

And there is much that must be learned to see the world in a new way—with clear eyes, with open ears and with real comprehension. This is the reformation, the reformation of yourself, your life, your mind, your experience, your feelings.

People clasp on to a spiritual idea or become attached to a spiritual teaching or teacher, and they try to live through this idea or through this relationship with this teaching and teacher, but they still must pass over the great bridge.

In doing this, you have the opportunity to make all the minor and major corrections that are necessary. You have the time to reconsider your life, and to choose again when that is necessary, and to revise your relationship with people, with places and things. All this revision is necessary for you to be able to be free to approach a new life and experience of being in the world.

It is taking this journey where you build strength, compassion for yourself and others and real self-determination that is not obsessive, that is not compulsive, that is not driven by your frightened, worldly mind.

This is why God has provided the bridge—the Steps to Knowledge, which has been studied before time even began in this world, throughout the universe, offered in many different forms, but all with the purpose of giving individuals the opportunity to escape the isolation, the confusion and the misery of Separation—not to take them out of the world, or their worlds, but to bring them back renewed, strengthened, complete and able to assume a real purpose and meaning in life.

THE POWER OF KNOWLEDGE

Here those who will journey up this mountain must leave those who merely philosophize or theorize or speculate or stand on the sidelines, trying to understand, or using theories and principles to try to comprehend what is beyond the reach of their intellect. Here the critics and the observers and the theorists stand at the bottom of the mountain, looking up, trying to comprehend, while those who are really called will begin to make the journey, setting out.

In setting out, you find that the journey is more complex and greater than you had anticipated. You cannot take everything with you. You cannot carry all these relationships with you. You cannot carry all these beliefs or feelings or regrets with you. You cannot be obsessing about your past because you are heading now into the future, a future that will be unlike the past. You cannot carry the burden of obsession, or even obligation, if you are to be free to set out on this journey.

Certain people will go with you. Certain people cannot. Circumstances may need to change, even dramatically over time. It all becomes apparent as you begin to climb this mountain, to pass over this great bridge.

It is you who change things. It is you who must be responsible for what you think, say and do. Never claim that you are being guided or that God told you to do something, for this is irresponsible. You must take full responsibility for your decisions here, and you must face the consequences of those decisions.

In this way, Heaven makes you powerful, gives you strength, determination and self-confidence, which you would not have if you thought you were just being guided, witlessly, moved around like a pawn in the world. That is not how this works at all, you see.

144

THE BRIDGE

You must become strong, competent, determined, capable, discerning and discreet. These are all qualities that must be built in time, and that is why the bridge is long and not short. You cannot enter the life you are meant to live in your current state of mind, with your strengths undeveloped and your weaknesses still dominating you.

God knows this, of course. From where you are, you can barely hear your inner nature. You can barely respond to Knowledge, you are so caught up and captivated by the outside and by your own internal difficulties. It is resolving these things and releasing that which must be released that you finally gain the strength, the freedom and the inspiration and confidence to move forward.

People will stay behind in their little prison cells, trying to make it more comfortable, redecorating their little space, trying to be distracted, trying to be pleased, trying to have enjoyable experiences as much as possible, unable to recognize that they are captive and cannot be fulfilled in that environment.

There is what people believe, and there is what God does. God does what works. People believe in what they want or what they try to reinforce so that they think their beliefs are the truth. Meanwhile, God does what works.

God moves through the world, working through individuals from the inside out—those who are free enough to respond, those who are responsible and can be strong and can take care of what is given them to do, without collapsing, without losing heart, without being drawn away or overtaken by the opinions of others.

THE POWER OF KNOWLEDGE

For God to work from the inside out with you, you must pass over this bridge. It is waiting for you. It has been waiting for you for a very long time, waiting for you to finally become honest enough with yourself and present to yourself sufficiently that you can realize that you need the power of redemption, that you are not living the life you were meant to live, that you are adrift and that none of your plans and schemes and thought-out beliefs will give you freedom from this.

It is here that you open yourself to the power of Knowledge within yourself and that you appeal to Heaven to help you. In this, Heaven will respond. You will begin a journey—the most important journey of your life, the greatest endeavor, the only thing that can fulfill you here in a world of confusion and distraction and tragedy.

CHAPTER 12

FOLLOWING THE PRESENCE

As revealed to
Marshall Vian Summers
on February 17, 2008
in Boulder, Colorado

There is a greater Mind within you, a greater Mind that the Creator
of all life has placed within you to guide you, to protect you and to
lead you to your greater accomplishments in life. This deeper Mind
is profoundly different from the mind that you think with—your
intellect, your worldly mind that has been conditioned and
formulated in response to the world and all the influences that come
from your family, your culture, your religion and so forth. But there
is a deeper Mind within you, the Mind of Knowledge.

This is where your deeper insights come from. This is where the
impulses come to hold you back from making bad decisions, from
committing yourself to relationships that have no future and no real
purpose. It is from Knowledge, then, that comes the real direction of
your life.

It has a plan already for your life, for you came into the world with
a greater purpose, with a specific mission to discover and to fulfill,
and with it the necessity of finding those individuals who will be
part of this mission and who will enable you to discover it and to
express it fully.

It is as if you have two entirely different agendas. You have your
personal agenda, which represents your goals and your plans and

147

THE POWER OF KNOWLEDGE

your values and the things that you think you must have to be safe
and secure and happy. Then you have a deeper agenda, an agenda
that was established before you came into the world—a goal, a gift,
a set of activities, a unique contribution to meet a specific need in
the world.

However, you live in your personal agenda, and that is constantly
being reinforced by the world around you, by your relationships, by
your activities, your habits and so forth. From the perspective of your
personal agenda, you cannot understand, you cannot figure out what
this deeper agenda is.

It is not your creation. It is not something you put together based
upon your fears, desires and preferences. It is something else entirely,
and it will seem profoundly mysterious to you, especially at the
outset. It is only by following this deeper agenda, by following the
presence of Knowledge, that you begin to discover how innately true
it is for you. And you will resonate with it ever more completely as
you proceed.

But beginning this journey can be very difficult and extremely
confusing, for you live within the context of your personal agenda:
your plans and your goals, your activities and your habits. You
identify yourself with these things and with the peculiarities of your
personality, your tastes, your preferences and everything else
regarding this you use to identify yourself, as if that is who you are,
as if you are only a body along with a collection of behaviors.

People identify with their thoughts, with their beliefs, thinking, "That
is who I am," and they call their thoughts and their beliefs the truth,
the truth for them, and sometimes they claim it is the truth for all
life. Some people even claim their ideas are God's truth. This, of

FOLLOWING THE PRESENCE

course, is ridiculous and extremely foolish and arrogant, but many people do assert this.

The real meaning of your spirituality is embedded in the deeper agenda within you. The purpose of your spirituality, the reality of your spirituality, are embedded in the deeper agenda within you that you carry like a secret cargo, undiscovered [while you are] still trying to live out your ideas and your preferences, still trying to accommodate yourself to the expectations of others, still seeking the approval of others, trying to survive in the outer world where everyone is trying to follow their personal agenda and where the culture itself establishes this agenda, gives it focus and goals, and controls it to a very great degree.

No matter how politically free you may be in your circumstances, if you have not begun to build a connection to the deeper agenda within you, you are really not free. You are still being governed by the dictates of your culture, the expectations of others, perhaps the beliefs of your primary religion. Even your personal agenda is mostly created for you by others. You build it and you absorb it from your environment, which you have been doing since the day you were born.

The world has been telling you who you are, and what you are, and what you must do, and what you must believe, and what you must not believe, and what you should associate yourself with, and what you should not associate yourself with. If you add religion onto that, well, then the dilemma becomes even deeper and more complicated.

But in spite of all of this, there is a greater reality within you, a greater Intelligence within you that is not conditioned by the world,

THE POWER OF KNOWLEDGE

that is not threatened by the world, that is not seeking approval and accommodation.

It is here on a mission. Its whole focus is to bring you into contact with this mission, to connect you with those people who will be significant and important within this mission, to bring you to the great need in the world that will call this mission out of you, for you cannot discover it yourself. It must be called out of you. It must be stimulated by a greater set of events. It is these that will connect you to the world and help you overcome your sense of isolation and separation.

But beginning the journey is difficult, and there are many significant thresholds along the way. At the outset, there must be something that brings to your awareness the reality that your current life is really not fulfilling something deep within you, that having more and more— more pleasure, more possessions, more stimulating activities, more escape from the world, more wealth, more power—all these things really are not satisfying something fundamental within you, and that there is something else.

You cannot define it. You may give it a name, but it is still mysterious as if something else is calling you or urging you or beckoning you. And everything else you are trying to do to fulfill your personal agenda is not satisfying this deeper need.

You look around you and you realize no one really knows who you are, except maybe one or two people, if you are very fortunate. And you do not really know who others are. It is a lot of movement without much meaning.

FOLLOWING THE PRESENCE

Trying to satisfy your personal agenda alone is unfulfilling. It leaves you empty and frustrated. Even if you are successful in meeting your goals, the success is short lived and fleeting.

Life is just a struggle here—a struggle to be, to do and to have, a struggle to keep away from danger and deprivation, poverty and misfortune. It is desperate and stressful.

At some point, through disappointment or disillusionment or some kind of meaningful encounter with another, the memory that you have a deeper mission in life is stimulated in some way, and you begin to gravitate towards it. Even taking very little, seemingly insignificant steps at the outset, you feel there is something else within you that you must discover, that you must come to know, that needs to be a part of your life, at least.

It is confusing because it does not fit within your personal agenda. It is something mysterious. It is not defined by the world. You try to give it a name and an explanation, but it remains mysterious nonetheless.

It is the Great Attraction of God. It is an attraction that is within you already because God put it there. You may formulate any belief about it. You may even take a very firm stance regarding your belief about it, but it is still greater than you. It still defies definition. You may claim your religion is the only true religion, but this within you is beyond your comprehension.

If you will begin to follow its attraction, its calling, if you can begin to create a place in your life for this, then you will begin to feel that there is a greater integrity within you. You will begin to gain a

THE POWER OF KNOWLEDGE

confidence that you could never have otherwise, not an arrogant confidence, but a confidence based upon a deeper association.

As you begin to take this greater journey, you reach thresholds along the way where you have to choose between something you want and something you really know; something you think you must have, or someone else says you must have, and something else in you that is leading you in a different direction. These are like gates on your journey. You come to this threshold, this gate, and you have to choose whether you will go through that gate and what you will follow within yourself.

These thresholds can be very significant. And particularly at the outset, and indeed all along the way, they deal with relationships with people, primarily. Your journey does not necessarily include the people that you have added to your life, or that you have become dependent upon, or that you think you must have, or whose expectations you feel you must fulfill.

With the exception of your children, whom you must take care of until they become adults, other relationships can become challenged by the power and the presence and the guidance of this Knowledge within you. This can lead to a great dilemma and a great challenge to you as to what you will honor in your life, what you will follow. It will reveal the degree to which you have accommodated yourself to other people, to which you have given away the authority of your life, the degree to which you have lost direction and have filled up your loneliness and your emptiness with others, who may not be able to make this great journey with you.

That is why it is so important to build your relationship with Knowledge first before you commit yourself to people and places,

152

FOLLOWING THE PRESENCE

careers and activities. This is what it means to seek the kingdom of God first, to build your connection and awareness of this deeper agenda within you.

If you can do this at first, then it creates a greater context for your relationships and informs you who you can be with and who you cannot be with, and how to be with those people whom you are meant to associate with. What is the appropriate form of your relationship? Over time, this will end all confusion about relationships and give you the necessary criteria that you will need to know who to be with and how to be with them appropriately so that the true meaning and value of your relationship can become revealed to both of you.

Without this deeper orientation, without this discernment, relationships are extremely risky and carry a great cost and weight with them. People are gambling their existence. They are gambling their freedom. They are gambling their lives, giving their lives away to people and situations that have no real promise for them, that are not really connected to the deeper criteria, the deeper agenda that exists within them that remains to be discovered.

People, of course, want to bargain and have everything. They do not want to give anything up. They want wealth and power and love, and they are afraid that all these things will be taken away. But the truth is that wealth and power and love are inherently destructive unless they are connected to the greater purpose that lives within you that you have brought into the world.

There is no prohibition against wealth, power and love if it is connected honestly to this deeper agenda within you, where it will be called upon and will be necessary. In fact, no one will really be able

153

THE POWER OF KNOWLEDGE

to carry out their greater purpose alone. They will need meaningful relationships in order to be successful because the Plan of God calls for the end of Separation to bring you out of isolation and fantasy, to free you from the prison of your own ideas, and the unhealthy associations you tend to make with others, and the obligations that will hold you back and prevent you from realizing your true nature and purpose here.

Your relationship with Knowledge represents your relationship with God. This is how God speaks to you. You may not hear this as a voice. It may be a feeling, an image, a sound, a voice. People experience the power and presence of Knowledge differently, according to their individual orientation.

But the truth remains that there is a greater agenda within you, a greater power within you, and it will provide the real relationships for you, the relationships of destiny. It will provide the true work and engagement in the world for you. It will give you power that the world does not understand, power that comes from within rather than is placed upon you from without.

This is what liberates you from confusion, ambivalence, condemnation, self-hatred and self-limiting beliefs and attitudes and habits. For if you follow this all the way, everything that is not true will be revealed to you and will fall away in time. Everything that does not represent your true life, your greater life and your greater purpose for being here will be revealed and will tend to fall away.

You will still be a person with weaknesses and unhealthy attractions perhaps. You will still be fallible. You will not be perfect. You will not be all powerful. But you will be following something that is all

FOLLOWING THE PRESENCE

powerful, that will give you strength and confidence, and will keep you from harming yourself and harming others.

You are connecting yourself now to something of the utmost importance that is central to your life, that is fulfilling the deeper need of your soul. You are still a person, and you are still fallible. You still have your weaknesses and your idiosyncrasies, but there is something else about you—a presence, a power, a commitment to life, a focus, an integrity that will impress and inspire others.

When someone has great presence, this is what it really means. It is not the force of their personality. It is not their self-assertion or their willpower. It is the presence that is with them, the presence of Knowledge. The deeper Mind within them has now become predominant, and their intellect, their personal worldly mind, is following and serving this greater power within them.

This is the real meaning of attaining a greater integrity. This is what it means to be true to oneself, which is being true to Knowledge, following the deeper agenda within one's life.

As We have said at the outset, it is all very confusing because the real power and authority is shifting gradually from the dominance of your personal mind and all of its overbearing beliefs and attitudes, commitments and condemnation of others, to a different kind of power within you. This shift happens gradually so that you can begin to adapt to it, to understand it and to learn from it.

For it is this transition from being outer directed to being inner directed, directed by Knowledge, that will teach you and give you the wisdom that you will need to be able to assist others and to fulfill your mission, which will require an understanding and a greater

THE POWER OF KNOWLEDGE

ability to recognize, experience and follow this greater power and this greater agenda within you.

Therefore, throughout this, you gain a necessary humility because you realize that you are dealing with something that is greater than you, but that requires your complete participation and that is relying upon your honesty and your integrity and your compassion and your love for people in the world.

It needs you as much as you need it. It changes you, but you cannot really change it. It illuminates your life, but it is already illuminated.

Perhaps in your life you are reaching one of the important thresholds where you have to choose again, where you have to make a real decision in life about what you will follow and what you will do. You have come to a gate in the journey, a gate that is waiting for you and that you must have the strength to open and to pass through.

Many people think they must rely upon the Power of God, but God must rely upon your strength and integrity because the gift from God to the world is coming through people. You are bringing to the world what the world cannot give itself, which is commitment and inspiration, which is compassion and care, which is creating that which is needed by people.

It is different from trying to fulfill one's desires and ambitions. Those are all part of the personal agenda that one has for oneself. This is really very different, you see. You cannot compare them.

When you come to one of these gates, you are not sure what is Knowledge and what is ambition. You are not sure you are making the right decision. There is a fork in the road. Which way will you

FOLLOWING THE PRESENCE

go? There are a lot of reasons why you want to go one way. There is the promise of wealth, of security, approval, social acceptance, recognition from others. But then the other way, none of these things seem to be really guaranteed. But there is something within you that is urging you to go there. Perhaps an opportunity has been presented to you, but within yourself, within Knowledge, it is not responding. If it is not a yes, it is a no. That is the certainty of Knowledge.

Sometimes there are conditions that must be established before you can agree to something. That is appropriate. That is fine. But it must be the right decision fundamentally. There is no bargaining here if you are really being true to yourself. You cannot make a deal and have it both ways. You cannot travel both routes if there is a fork in the road.

You cannot take people with you who are not willing to go, who do not feel this calling, who do not have a natural affinity with it. Perhaps it is not their time and their place to feel the power of Knowledge within themselves.

It will strengthen you immensely to choose Knowledge over other things that appear to be attractive and are even thought to be necessary. Again, it is part of the shifting of authority within yourself from your ideas to Knowledge itself, from your beliefs and expectations to Knowledge itself, from your fears and insecurity to Knowledge itself.

This is how God saves you. This is how God redeems you—by placing within you a greater voice and a greater purpose that you can only learn to respond to and to follow as clearly and as honestly as you can. At the end of life, God does not simply dispel this world,

THE POWER OF KNOWLEDGE

dispel your worldly consciousness because that is who you think you are.

You are fulfilled and redeemed by carrying out the greater purpose that has brought you into the world. This is how the Separation is ended. This is how you regain your fundamental relationship with God and with your Spiritual Family—those who have been called to support and assist you, both within the world and beyond.

There is no final Judgment Day. That is ridiculous. God knows that without Knowledge, you can only make mistakes in this life. You will live a life of compromise and frustration, anger and resentment. Your soul's need will be unmet. You will be dissatisfied. You will blame others and the world for your dissatisfaction. You will be unhappy fundamentally. No matter how pleasant your surroundings, no matter how much wealth you may acquire, you will be fundamentally dissatisfied because you have not fulfilled your greater purpose for coming into the world. You have given yourself away to other things. You have been seduced by the world.

But this does not make God angry because without Knowledge, you can only be seduced by the world. You can only create some other identity for yourself and try to live out your personal agenda, which has largely been created for you by the influences around you.

Your redemption comes from taking the Steps to Knowledge and by following the guidance and the direction of Knowledge as faithfully and patiently and honestly as you can. This is eminently practical because it leads to fundamental action.

It is not like you are having a romance with the Angelic Presence. It is not like you are just indulging yourself in ecstasy. That is really not

158

FOLLOWING THE PRESENCE

the journey, you see, because you came to the world to work, to accomplish something, to find certain people and to accomplish something with them in meeting a real need in the world.

This is not a path of personal fulfillment where you find the most pleasant thing to do in life and you give yourself to that. That just leads to greater frustration and greater misery, for it does not meet the need of the soul. This is not a selfish indulgence. This is not where you become irresponsible to others and commit yourself to your own happiness and success. That is your personal agenda. Knowledge is here to bring you into service to people and to the world, to connect you with people in the world through meaningful activity and contribution.

People are very confused about the goal and purpose of religion and spirituality. They think it is either some kind of subservience to a foreign god, or they think it is the path of personal happiness and personal satisfaction. From their personal agenda and their personal mind, they cannot see the real movement of God in the world, the real movement of Knowledge within the individual and between individuals. They think it is something else. They cannot see it from where they are.

Just like from the boat on the water, you cannot see the deeper currents that are moving water all over the planet. You can only see the turbulence of the surface and the effect of the weather upon the wave. You can only comprehend the mystery and the meaning and the power of Knowledge by becoming engaged with it, by following it and not trying to control it or define it or manipulate it to fulfill your interests or desires.

THE POWER OF KNOWLEDGE

Some people think, "Well, you surrender yourself to God and God takes over," but it is not really like that, for you must still be the captain of your ship. You still must direct your thoughts and your actions and establish criteria for your relationships and boundaries for yourself.

The difference here is that Knowledge is guiding you, and you are responding to it. It is holding you back from doing things that would lead you astray, and it is urging you on in a certain direction, relentlessly. You are still the captain of your ship, you see. The difference is now you are responding to the real purpose of your journey, where the ship really must go and what it contains.

People are immensely confused because they have not really begun the journey, or they have not traveled on it far enough to realize what it is and how it works and the mystery and the miracle that it produces in the lives of those who can respond.

At the outset, there are many difficult decisions to be made. They are fundamental in determining whether you will be a free person in this life or not. They are fundamental in determining whether you can respond and experience and fulfill a greater purpose in your life, or whether you will merely be a captive to the expectations of others and to your own insecurity and sense of inadequacy.

Even as you begin to travel along the way, even halfway up this great mountain, there are other challenges as well. For you still have a personal agenda going with you. It does not get left behind at the foot of the mountain. You take it with you, and it is still operative, and you still must make decisions regarding it.

FOLLOWING THE PRESENCE

Your intellect was created to make small decisions, to function within the constantly changing circumstances of your life. But Knowledge is there to give you purpose, meaning and direction and to give you a greater reference point within yourself, to be able to discern what is true and what is untrue, what is good from what only looks good, what is really advantageous from what is merely seductive, what is real honesty from what is real dishonesty. It is your deeper reference point, you see.

You still must use your mind to make decisions and to carry out the innumerable tasks of daily life, but now you have a greater reference point. It is like a beacon. You now can go to what is wise within you for counsel, to seek direction, to help you make important decisions, whereas before you were just recklessly guessing, hoping and wishing, without any real source or sense of security or certainty within yourself.

This is the difference that will make all the difference in your life: whether this life will be a fulfillment of the greater purpose that has sent you here, and those who have sent you here, and the power and presence that you carry; or will it be a wasted existence by someone who is simply trying to be comfortable in an uncomfortable world, who is just hanging on to what little they have, who lives in fear and apprehension and has no real power or sense of inner direction?

Many people live and will fall into this latter category. Some of them merely are held back by their circumstances, by their poverty or political oppression. They have no freedom of movement from where they are. They are locked in place.

But for others who have these freedoms, it is truly tragic if they neglect to discover and to experience and to fulfill the greater

THE POWER OF KNOWLEDGE

purpose within them, the deeper agenda that exists within them. Their lives are truly wasted, chasing pleasure and avoiding pain. They are a slave to other forces, and their real life and real value are unknown to them.

You do not want to be amongst their number, for you have a greater purpose in being here. You cannot define it. You cannot control it. But you can follow it. It is giving you signs and cues as you go along. It will change your values, your priorities. You will seek quiet more than stimulation. You will seek honest and meaningful conversation with others instead of mere chatter. You will seek inspiration instead of just stimulation. You will seek a deeper inner resonance over mere excitement on the outside.

This is entirely natural. This is coming home to yourself. This is allowing your values and your thoughts to change because you are experiencing something fundamental now. Your values are becoming more in line with your true nature. And with it, there will be greater self-acceptance.

But you must journey on. There are many temptations to set up permanent camp on the side of this mountain, but you must continue because you will not see and you will not know until you reach its greater and higher elevations, where you can see your life and the reality of life around you without obstruction.

And you have to leave behind certain people, even wonderful people, who cannot make the journey with you. It is not their time. They are not ready. It may not even be their way up the mountain that you must follow. Others will come to join you, and you will have a deeper resonance with them. Some will travel with you temporarily; some will make the entire journey with you. Only Knowledge knows.

FOLLOWING THE PRESENCE

This is following the presence of Knowledge. This is following the Presence of God. This is learning how to be in the world but not of the world. This is learning how to build a connection to your Ancient Home while you are here, living a fundamental and practical life engaged with others in meaningful activities.

This is the journey before you. This is what it means to take the Steps to Knowledge. This is what it means to live a greater reality even while you are here engaged in daily life in the world. This is where the Divine expresses itself through the mundane and gives the mundane all the meaning and value that it has.

This is what gives real purpose to your intellect. This is what influences you to live a healthy and constructive life. This is what sets you on firm and established ground, a firm foundation in the world, a foundation that the world itself can never provide for you. For you are born of a Greater Reality from which you have come and to which you will return. This holds the secret, the purpose and the real value of your life.

CHAPTER 13

THE SPIRITUAL FIRE

As revealed to
Marshall Vian Summers
on February 23, 2013
in Boulder, Colorado

Within you, deep within you, beneath the surface of the mind, in a place you barely know, there is a Fire, a spiritual Fire. It is the source of your inspiration. It is the Fire of Knowledge, the deeper Mind within you, burning like a hearth, consuming your errors and your pain, purifying you, blessing you, guiding you.

But you are far away from this hearth—living at the surface, the turbulent surface of your mind; living at the surface of the world, with all of its tragedies, inducements and misfortunes; busy, caught up in things, stimulated but agitated, driven on by your life and your needs and your possessions and the requirements of others. You do not feel this Fire, though it is burning within you.

As a creature of the Earth, your heart will continue to beat, your body will work. But these things cannot produce the desire to create, the desire to establish true relationships, the desire for meaning and the search for meaning. These must come from a deeper incentive that lives within you, deep down within you.

This comes from the Fire, for the Fire is the engine of your greater life. It is generating a greater incentive beyond merely surviving and indulging in things in this world. It produces a search for meaning beyond comfort and security. It takes you farther than you would go

165

THE POWER OF KNOWLEDGE

otherwise. It challenges you. It seeks to have you go further, beyond this point, even beyond whatever success you feel you must have for yourself. To assure your happiness and safety in the world, there is this greater Fire urging you to a higher purpose and calling in life.

How will you know this Fire is there? Because when you become still, when you sit quietly, you can feel it. It does not reside only in one part of your body, but you can feel it in your heart and in your stomach. You can feel the pressure to seek that which is calling for you in the world.

You cannot be comfortable with comfort alone. You cannot be self-assured with all the trappings of security. You cannot be satisfied with little things because the Fire is there. It is mysterious. You cannot conceptualize it. You cannot use it for your own intentions. You cannot use it to gain wealth or privilege or to win over others. The Fire has its own purpose. It has greater plans for your life.

Here Knowledge is not merely a concept or an imagined thing. It is a visceral reality. You can feel it in your body. It is the source of your life force here. It is powerful. It is subtle. If you were to come into its proximity, you would see how strong it really is and how it illuminates the landscape within you.

But far away, it is a single point of light, a flickering light on the horizon within yourself. You cannot yet feel its warmth, its power, its encouragement and its direction. For you are lost in the world— caught up in the world, caught up in your mind, which is caught up in the world; fascinated and frightened by the things around you, over-stimulated and over-involved. Your mind is dominating your attention. Your activities are using up all of your time. So the Fire is barely felt, except in moments of sobriety or repose. You can

THE SPIRITUAL FIRE

feel there is something in you—the source of your energy, your greater energy.

You are going to need this Fire. You are going to need this Fire to face a world of increasing environmental, social and economic instability. You are going to need this Fire to face the rising uncertainty in people around you. You are going to need this Fire to build the Four Pillars of your life—the Pillar of Relationships, the Pillar of Health, the Pillar of Work and Providership and the Pillar of Spiritual Development. These are the Pillars that uphold your life and will give you strength to endure hardship and the great change that is coming to the world.

You need this Fire to prevent yourself from falling into despair or from becoming jaded and cynical. You need this Fire to keep your eyes open, to keep listening, looking and watching the horizon of your life. You will need this Fire to find those people who hold a key to your greater work and relationships in life.

For if you live only at the surface of your mind, you will perish there. You will lose your direction. You will lose your incentive. You will lose your passion for life. You will lose your inspiration. And you will fall into despair. Even if you live with affluence and luxury, you will fall into despair.

God has given you Knowledge to guide you, to bless you, to protect you and to prepare you for a greater life of fulfillment and contribution in the world. This Knowledge has a fire, a power and a potency to it. Strong enough it is to overcome your inhibition, to move you to do certain things or to hold you back from things that would harm you, distract you or lead your life in a dangerous direction.

THE POWER OF KNOWLEDGE

More powerful than your ideas it is. More powerful than your fixed beliefs, more powerful than all of the fixed beliefs in the world put together is the power of Knowledge within you. And this Fire is its power. For it is the Fire of love. It is the Fire of courage. It is the Fire of determination. It is the Fire of compassion and forgiveness. It is the Fire that purifies all things that are impure and harmful within you.

When you begin to take the Steps to Knowledge and to learn how to feel your life beneath the surface of your mind, you will begin to feel the warmth and the strength and the potency of this Fire. It will give you courage. It will restore you. And it will take you away from your fear and anxiety. It will show you that everyone with whom you have grievances is actually teaching you to value this Knowledge and to reach for this Fire.

This is your freedom, you see, for nothing in the world can extinguish this. And it remains pure within you. Even if your life has been defiled, even if your life has been misspent, even if your life is currently suffering under subjugation or oppression by others, the Fire is pure within you. It will give you the eyes to see and the ears to hear and the strength to look at life objectively. It will restore you from your obsessions and addictions, for it is more powerful than they.

God has not only given you the wisdom. God has given you the Fire to realize and to live this wisdom. If you sit quietly, you can begin to feel it once your mind settles down. It is really so close to you, but you are looking in another direction. Your mind is elsewhere—caught up in things, caught up in the future, caught up in the past.

THE SPIRITUAL FIRE

With this Fire, you will feel the Presence that abides with you, the Presence of those who watch over you, the Presence that this sacred Fire maintains within you—the Fire that cannot be extinguished, for it was burning before you came into this world, and it will be burning once you leave this place.

Rich or poor, no matter what the circumstances of your life or the dilemmas or difficulties facing you at this moment, you can return to the Fire. Your redemption is so close, but it will take time for you to bring this awareness into your life, to establish the practices that are necessary for you to engage with your deeper nature and to benefit from the greater strength that God has given you.

For God is not directing your life and managing your affairs. God has given you the power of Knowledge to give you true direction and purpose in a chaotic world. You were born with it. It is with you now. And it will be with you when you leave this place. What greater gift can God give you?

The world is chaotic. Do not think everything serves a higher purpose. Do not think everything is divinely guided, for God set in motion the biological, geological and evolutionary forces at the beginning of time, and these are working on their own. Therefore, change is unpredictable. Everything can change in a moment. Your mistakes or others' mistakes can alter the course of your life. Tragedy can occur. Nothing is assured except the power of Knowledge within you.

When you come to realize this, you will turn to Heaven and to the strength that Heaven has given you. This will be the great turning point—when you see that the only real security you have in this world is the power of Knowledge within you and the strength of your

THE POWER OF KNOWLEDGE

relationships and the degree to which you have built the Four Pillars of your life.

Beyond this, everything is ideas and speculation, fantasy and belief. But belief has little power against the forces of change in the world. And God has given you a greater strength to call upon in every avenue of your life.

When you realize that the substitutes for this power cannot assure your safety or your success, you will turn to the strength that Heaven has bestowed upon you—a Wisdom, a Presence and a Fire. You cannot imagine how important this is for you and how this can guide your decisions and free you from ambivalence and confusion that are so pervasive.

This is why people have such strong and fixed beliefs because underneath this they are afraid and confused. And the more afraid and confused, the more they attach themselves to their ideas or to their associations in life with dogged and stupid perseverance. They cannot see beyond the prison house they have created for themselves. They have locked themselves indoors. They cannot see the sunrise. They cannot see the mystery of their life. This is not your fate.

Do not look for intellectual confirmation, for this is weak and changeable with little foundation in the world. God has given you the greater strength. The task now is to take the Steps to Knowledge, for this is the essence of all spiritual practice, given now in God's New Revelation in a pure form that has never been altered or accommodated by people over time.

Your task is to engage with the power and presence of Knowledge and to bring resolution to your outer life, for it is draining you of

THE SPIRITUAL FIRE

time and energy and resources. Your task now is to take the Steps to Knowledge to find the greater power and to feel this power, which is the Fire of Knowledge within you.

This is not the fire of passionate belief. This is not the fire of admonition. This is not the fire of an angry God casting down the nations. Release these ideas, for they are born of human ignorance and condemnation. An angry God is the projection and creation of angry people.

The power that God has given you is gracious, but potent. It is determined. You cannot bargain with it. You can only receive it and respond to its gifts and its direction as you navigate an increasingly difficult and conflicted world.

The Light of Revelation lives in a place within you you have forgotten in your journey in the world, in a place where you are safe and have assurance of your future. For this is the part of you that cannot be destroyed and cannot be corrupted. It is the Light of hope for those who are oppressed. It is the Light of upliftment for those who are depressed. It is the strength for those who seemingly have no power in the world. It is the gift of life for those who have acquired too much, whose lives have gone stagnant amongst their possessions. It is the resolution, you see, for God put the answer in you before the questions have even arisen.

No matter what your predicament, God has put the power that can take you out of the jungle of confusion. And the Fire burns. Once it is felt, once it is recognized, it cannot be forgotten. Once its gifts have been received, it will set in motion a process of re-evaluation in your life as the false gods begin to fail. It will restore you and redeem you

171

THE POWER OF KNOWLEDGE

over time as you learn to follow its guidance and to become a vehicle of its expression in the world.

This is the Fire that transcends religious belief and ideology. It is there for everyone—the Christian, the Buddhist, the Muslim, the Jew and all other forms of religious practice and understanding. It is recognized in certain traditions. It is called a "god" in certain traditions of the past—the fire god, the god of fire—because fire is power, fire is restoration, fire is survival, fire is warmth. But this is a different kind of Fire. This Fire does not destroy. This Fire does not burn your house down. This Fire does not singe and harm your body. This is the spiritual Fire, you see. It consumes that which is impure.

Give, then, your fear to this Fire. Give your ambivalence to this Fire. Give your sense of oppression to this Fire. Give your anger, your hatred and your condemnation to this Fire. See yourself sitting near it and feeding these things into it, for it will purify all things that are untrue.

God's New Revelation for the world brings clearly forth the power of redemption for the individual and the greater hope for the world. For if the power of Knowledge within the individual cannot be ignited, there is no hope for the world. Humanity will follow its desperate and destructive course with inevitable outcome, and the world will be damaged to such a point that it can barely sustain a human population. Such is the product of human greed, corruption and ignorance.

It is the Fire now that is more essential than ever. It is not merely for your personal redemption. It is for the restoration of the world, to prepare humanity to live in a new world and to face a universe, a

THE SPIRITUAL FIRE

Greater Community of life, that will alter the course of human destiny and the future of every person.

You may feel hopeless, but hope lives within you. You may feel helpless, but strength lives within you. You may feel oppressed by your circumstances, but a greater life lives within you, waiting to be received, expressed and discovered.

Come, then, to the Fire. Come, then, to that which warms you, gives you strength, courage and restores to you your dignity and purpose for being in the world. This is the blessing. This is the offering. This is how God brings you back and gives you a greater life in this world.

CHAPTER 14

THE REMEMBRANCE

As revealed to
Marshall Vian Summers
on March 12, 2016
in Boulder, Colorado

You carry within you the memory of your Ancient Home, deep beneath the surface of your mind, deep beneath the surface of that part of your mind that has been conditioned by the world and is fixated upon the world. But deeper within you, there is a greater remembrance, there is a greater Presence, there is a greater connection with your Spiritual Family beyond this world, who have sent you here, on a mission, with a purpose to fulfill.

You have not lost your connection to Heaven. In fact, you are tethered to Heaven even while you wander in the universe, living in Separation, living in Separation from all that truly is that is permanent and timeless and forever. But what is timeless and forever is not what your eyes see, or your ears hear, or what your hands can touch.

For you are living in a different kind of reality now, a temporary reality—temporary on a long time scale. It has a beginning, a middle and an end. And at this moment, you are somewhere in the middle, for the end is far ahead of you, and the beginning is far behind you.

You are like the iceberg, you see. Part of it is above the water line, but much of it is beneath, out of sight, hidden, but still completely part of the structure of who you are. And, in fact, it is the ballast to

THE POWER OF KNOWLEDGE

who you are. It is the foundation of who you are. It is who you are, in timeless reality.

But here in this world, at this time, you are a person. You are a singular identity—part of a culture, part of a nation, part of the events of this world at this time, conditioned by this world, fixated upon this world, dominated by this world.

But deep beneath the water line, deep beneath the surface of your mind, there is the power of Knowledge, the deeper Mind within you. And this Knowledge holds the remembrance of your Ancient Home.

At some point, perhaps in a moment of despair or great sobriety about your life, or a moment of great prescience and clarity of mind, you will feel this remembrance. It is not something that you will recall in images. It is more a deeper feeling of connection, what it felt like to be there, and how different that is from where you are now—a completely different reality, most assuredly. And perhaps in these moments of greater clarity, where you are not obsessed with the world or yourself, you will feel these things, for they live within you at every moment. You cannot lose them, really. Even though you are wandering in time and space, they are with you always.

And when you leave this life, you will return to the remembrance and to those who sent you into the world, with great clarity of what you were sent here to do and great certainty of whether you did it or not. There is no punishment here, you see. There is no damnation, for that is a human creation. There is only the remembrance. "Ah, yes, I was in that world, in that place."

But here, at this moment, the remembrance is so important because it begins to restore to you—consciously—your connection to

THE REMEMBRANCE

Heaven, and with this connection, you have a lifeline feeding you strength and purpose, strength and courage.

Before this, you are a product of your culture as if you were remade within this culture—dominated by others, your family, your friends, society's expectations, dominated even by the physical forces in your body.

But now the other great portion of your life begins to emerge in your awareness. You are no longer just the tip of the iceberg above the water line. You are becoming something deeper, stronger and greater—more substantial in the world than this frail creature that you are today, more independent, less affected by the turbulent and tragic world around you, less drawn by desire and less discouraged by catastrophe.

God has sent the New Revelation into the world for this time and for the times to come. It brings to you the gateway to remembrance through taking the Steps to Knowledge, engaging your worldly mind with the deeper Mind, the immortal Mind, within you. And with this comes, in little increments perhaps, here and there, the remembrance of your Ancient Home, in feeling.

You do not remember what it looks like because what it looks like is not how this reality is portrayed. But you remember being with certain individuals and presences with the immediate and clear understanding of what you are doing and why you are coming into the world. This is all part of the remembrance.

Beyond this is Creation itself, timeless, inconceivable from where you stand today. Anything that is immortal is inconceivable to a mind that has been created in time and space. That is why you

177

THE POWER OF KNOWLEDGE

cannot conceive of Heaven. Or if you try, as many people do, it becomes kind of an extension of your life in the world, only much better of course, but ultimately extremely boring and uneventful. For if life is good all the time, it ceases to be a pleasant experience.

But your Ancient Home is entirely different from this, you see, and that is why you cannot imagine it. But you can feel the power and presence of Knowledge within you: a Mind born of Heaven, a part of you that has never left God, your lifeline to Heaven and in this world, in this life, the foundation of your strength, your integrity and the keeper of the greater purpose that has brought you here, and with it the remembrance and the recognition of those who in life will play a necessary role in the expression of this purpose.

What greater strength could God give to you than the remembrance? For with it comes the strength of your immortality, which begins to unravel the countless layers of fear, apprehension, resentment and unforgiveness that are so much a part of your experience living in Separation.

What greater gift could God give you than the remembrance of who you are, why you came, who sent you and what it means to be in the world, living with a greater purpose and mission for being here?

As you take the Steps to Knowledge, as you begin to allow Knowledge to reshape your life and the remembrance to give you its strength, courage and integrity, you will look at others as if they are living in chains—bound to their ideas, lost in their fears and their fantasies, believing in their delusions, trying to be happy, trying to be comfortable, trying to be secure but always feeling insecure, always feeling uncomfortable, always driven by anxiety.

THE REMEMBRANCE

Their plight, which was your plight before, now becomes ever clearer, and you will look upon them with compassion, for you will see their dilemma more clearly. You will see more clearly the reality of living in Separation, apart from your Ancient Home and all that existed there. But now you have begun the remembrance slowly, surely, as your life begins to become simple and clear, as your mind begins to open from its long and troubled dream of Separation.

It is the remembrance. It is the feeling that you are not alone. There is the recognition that you are not really lost, lost as you were before. There is something more solid and permanent within you now that transcends belief and ideology.

You can feel it, and as you feel it, it becomes stronger and more prevalent in your life, providing contrast and giving you freedom from constant anxiety and self-repudiation. Your values change. Your priorities change, naturally, because you are beginning to remember.

As you remember, you feel Heaven smiling upon you, and your old fear of God, your old fear of punishment, your old fear of sin, your old fear of being exposed to the Presence begins to melt away. Like ice upon the pond, in the warmth of Heaven, it begins to melt away.

Now you have an anchor for being in the world that is not of the world but that must be in the world. For you are not of the world, but now you must be in the world. But you need this anchor, you see, or you will be adrift—adrift on the turbulent seas of the world, lost, drifting, unknown to yourself and others.

But now you have sails and you have direction. Now your life can begin to move as it was meant to move, as it was designed to move, as it was intended to move. Slowly, moments here and there, you feel it.

THE POWER OF KNOWLEDGE

But the moments increase as you take the Steps to Knowledge. As you allow your mind to settle down; as you learn how to live without constant fear and uncertainty; as you find freedom each day from self-repudiation and self-doubt; as you are freed from unhealthy engagements with others, unhealthy habits within your own thinking and behavior, the moments of remembrance increase, become more pervasive, become more like the background of your real life. Instead of only a fleeting moment here and there, it becomes the ground underneath your feet, the ballast for your ship so that it can withstand the winds of the world and sail the turbulent seas with assurance.

What could God give you that would be greater than this? Wealth? Romance? To deepen your engagement with Separation, to deepen your attachment to things that have no meaning or value?

How could God give you peace of mind if you had no idea of who you are? Or why you are here? Or what you must do? Or where you must go? What reassurance could God really give you beyond the power of Knowledge and the remembrance?

As you climb this mountain, your fear of Heaven will disappear. Your fear of death will begin to fade away. Now, as you proceed, it is your direction that is important, and you do not want that to be threatened or destroyed.

Your future in Heaven is assured. There will be no Hell and damnation. But your success in this life is dependent upon the recognition and the fulfillment of your mission, and discovering those individuals who will play a significant and necessary role here.

THE REMEMBRANCE

This will become your focus. The fear that lives within you, then, is the fear that you may not be able to fulfill this mission, or that you may become distracted as you were before, or that your life may break down, or your health may collapse.

Your emphasis here is entirely different. Now your emphasis is on following the direction with growing understanding of what it is and what it is not, where it must go and where it must not go, who it involves and who it does not involve. You see, it is not just a definition. It is clearing away that which does not belong, that which is not you, that which attached itself to you or that you attached to yourself in your previous life.

As these things fall away, and as you come into the clear, then your direction becomes more evident, more certain, more substantial. It is not just the end point that is important. It is the discovery, for this is what undoes Separation within you—finally liberating you from the chains of Separation, finally giving you the eyes to see and the ears to hear, finally giving you true relationship. For with the remembrance comes the experience of true relationship.

Even if you are entirely alone and have not found your true companions in the world, you will feel that you are known and supported, that your life is valued, for reasons that you cannot invent but which live intrinsically within you. You will know this with the remembrance, and the remembrance will grow as you proceed in receiving God's great Revelation for the world.

For while all the previous Revelations brought the remembrance, they were changed by man, overlaid with customs and traditions that had nothing to do with the original intent of Revelation. They became the culture. They became the state. They became everyone's

THE POWER OF KNOWLEDGE

ideas. And the remembrance was lost, except by those who could see beyond all of these things and hold to the true Revelations as they were given in previous times.

But now you are hearing the Revelation uncontaminated, unchanged by man, unadulterated, without culture and politics, and human will and greed and corruption to muddy the stream. For here the waters are clear and pure, and the Will of Heaven is evident within them. This gives you the greatest opportunity to find your way and to escape your troubled past and to begin to experience the remembrance.

For how can you not remember where you have lived [eternally]? How can you not remember what that felt like? How can you not remember those who sent you into the world, who represent your working group, your Spiritual Family? Your current existence is like a grain of sand, and your true existence is like the beach that stretches as far as the eye can see. How can you not remember such a great thing?

The truth is you can, and you will. But you must have the correct preparation. You must have the right approach. You must have the right instruction. And you must have relationships in life here that can support this and reflect this for you.

So the Messenger calls those to gather with him at certain times so that he can impart the Presence and the Remembrance and so that you, who feel so called, can recognize you are not alone and that relationships of true meaning are there, not just in one person only, but all around you, as you gather in the Circle of the Messenger. This is all part of the Remembrance, you see.

182

THE REMEMBRANCE

For the power and persuasions of the world are very strong, very dominating, so dominating they can overshadow the remembrance, as they have for everyone here until they begin to awaken.

So God must give the pathway. God must give the [Messenger]. God must remind you repeatedly, over and over again, of what lives deep within you, beyond the surface of your mind: the remembrance of that, and with that the remembrance that you have come from a Greater Reality, to which you will return at some point, when your work here is done, when your service to those who remain behind is fulfilled sufficiently.

And you will carry this beyond this world to join those who watch over the world. For you do not simply die and go to Heaven. You join those who support everyone who remains behind—your Spiritual Family, your working group. They are like streams that join with other streams in time, which join with rivers, which become great rivers, which lead to the great ocean of God's Love and Power and Presence.

You are blessed because the Revelation is known to you. You are blessed because Knowledge lives within you, and it remains uncontaminated by the world, and is unafraid of the world, and is not confused about anything that confuses you today. And you are blessed because the memory of your Ancient Home and of those who sent you into the world are with you, always.

Take then now the steps towards remembrance. Take then now the Steps to Knowledge. Receive in humility and in gratitude the Revelation for this time and the times to come.

THE POWER OF KNOWLEDGE

Let your heart and your deeper sense enable you to respond. Allow your mind to be confused, for it is confused already. Allow things to be undefined until Knowledge can make life clear to you over time. Allow your journey to open before you, step by step, rather than constructing some belief about what it is and what it will mean.

You control yourself in taking the journey. You will need to control your mind and emotions and involvements with others, and bring greater clarity and discernment to these things.

But the journey itself is being given to you from beyond you. For you do not know your way to return. Nor can you construct it for yourself.

It is mysterious, just like the remembrance, just like Knowledge within you, just like the greater reality of you that lives beneath the water line, beneath the surface of the mind.

Important Terms

The New Message from God reveals that our world stands at the greatest threshold in the history and evolution of humanity. At this threshold, God has spoken again, revealing the great change that is coming to the world and our destiny within the Greater Community of life beyond our world, for which we are unaware and unprepared.

Here the Revelation redefines certain familiar terms, but within a greater context and introduces other terms that are new to the human family. It is important to understand these terms when reading the texts of the New Message and hearing the Voice of Revelation.

GOD is revealed in the New Message as the Source and Creator of all life and of countless races in the universe. Here the greater reality of God is unveiled in the expanded context of life in this world and all life in the universe. This greater context redefines the meaning of our understanding of God and of God's Power and Presence in our lives. The New Message states that to understand what God is doing in our world, we must understand what God is doing in the entire universe. This is now being revealed for the first time through a New Message from God. In the New Message, God is not a divine entity, personage or a singular awareness, but instead a pervasive force and presence that permeates all life and is moving all life in the universe towards a state of unity. God speaks to the deepest part of each person through the power of Knowledge that lives within them.

THE SEPARATION is the ongoing state and condition of being separate from God. The Separation began when part of Creation willed to have the freedom to be apart from God, to live in a state of

THE POWER OF KNOWLEDGE

Separation. As a result, God created our evolving world and the expanding universe as a place for the separated to live in countless forms and places. Before the Separation, all life was in a timeless state of pure union. It is to this original state of union with God that all those living in Separation are ultimately called to return—through relationship, service and the discovery of Knowledge. It is God's mission in our world and throughout the universe to reclaim the separated through Knowledge, which is the part of each individual still connected to God.

KNOWLEDGE is the deeper spiritual Intelligence within each person, waiting to be discovered. Knowledge represents the eternal part of us that has never left God. The New Message speaks of Knowledge as the great hope for humanity, an inner power at the heart of each person that God's New Message is here to reveal and to call forth. This deeper spiritual Intelligence exists beyond our thinking mind and the boundaries of our intellect. It alone has the power to guide each of us to our higher purpose and destined relationships in life. The New Message teaches extensively about the reality and experience of Knowledge.

THE ANGELIC ASSEMBLY is the presence of God's Angels who have been assigned to watch over our world and the evolution of humanity. This Assembly is part of the hierarchy established by God to support the redemption and return of all those living in Separation in the physical reality. Every world where sentient life exists is watched over by an Angelic Assembly. The Assembly overseeing our world is now translating the Will of God for our time into human language and understanding, which is now being revealed through the New Message from God. The term Angelic Assembly is synonymous with the terms Angelic Presence and Angelic Host in the text of the New Message.

186

IMPORTANT TERMS

THE NEW MESSAGE FROM GOD is a communication from God to people of all nations and religions. It represents the next stage of God's progressive Revelation for the human family and comes in response to the great challenges and needs of humanity today. The New Message is over 9000 pages in length and is the largest Revelation ever given to the world, given now to a literate world of global communication and growing global awareness. The New Message is not an offshoot or reformation of any past tradition and is not given for one tribe, nation or group alone. It is God's New Message for the whole world, which is now facing Great Waves of environmental, social and political change and the new threshold of emerging into a Greater Community of intelligent life in the universe.

THE VOICE OF REVELATION is the united voice of the Angelic Assembly delivering God's Message through a Messenger sent into the world for this task. Here the Assembly speaks as one Voice, the many speaking as one. For the first time in history, you are able to hear the actual Voice of Revelation speaking through God's Messenger. It is this Voice that has spoken to all God's Messengers in the past. The Word and the Sound of the Voice of Revelation are in the world and are available for you to hear in their original audio form.

THE MESSENGER is the one chosen, prepared and sent into the world by the Angelic Assembly to receive the New Message from God. The Messenger for this time is Marshall Vian Summers. Marshall is a humble man with no position in the world who has undergone a long and difficult preparation to receive God's New Revelation and bring it to the world. He is charged with the great burden, blessing and responsibility of presenting this Revelation to a divided and conflicted world. He is the first of God's Messengers to

THE POWER OF KNOWLEDGE

reveal the reality of a Greater Community of intelligent life in the universe. The Messenger has been engaged in this process of Revelation since the year 1982.

THE PRESENCE refers to different but interconnected realities: the presence of Knowledge within the individual, the Presence of the Angelic Assembly that oversees the world or ultimately the Presence of God in the universe. The Presence of these three realities offers a life-changing experience of grace and relationship. All three are connected to the larger process of growth and redemption for us, for the world and for the universe at large. Together they represent the mystery and purpose of our lives, which the New Message reveals to us in the clearest possible terms. The New Revelation offers a modern pathway for experiencing the power of the Presence in your life.

STEPS TO KNOWLEDGE is an ancient book of spiritual practice now being given by God to the world for the first time. Steps provides the lessons and practices necessary for learning and living the New Message from God. In beginning the Steps, you embark on a journey of discovering Knowledge, the mysterious source of your inner power and authority, and with it the essential relationships you are destined to find. Its 365 daily "steps," or practices, lead you to a personal revelation about your life and destiny. In taking this greater journey, you can discover the power of Knowledge and your experience of profound inner knowing, which lead you to your higher purpose and calling in life.

THE GREATER COMMUNITY is the larger universe of intelligent life in which our world has always existed. This Greater Community encompasses all worlds in the universe where sentient life exists, in all states of evolution and development. The New Message reveals that humanity is in an early and adolescent phase of

IMPORTANT TERMS

its development and that the time has now come for humanity's emergence into the Greater Community. It is here, standing at the threshold of space, that humanity discovers that it is not alone in the universe, or even within its own world.

THE GREATER COMMUNITY WAY OF KNOWLEDGE is a timeless tradition representing God's work in the universe to reclaim the separated in all worlds through the power of Knowledge that is inherent in all intelligent life. To understand what God is doing in our world, we must begin to understand what God is doing in the entire universe. For the first time in history, The Greater Community Way of Knowledge is being presented to the world through a New Message from God. The New Message opens the portal to this timeless work of God underway throughout the universe in which we live. We stand at the threshold of emerging into this Greater Community and must now have access to The Greater Community Way of Knowledge in order to understand our destiny as a race and successfully navigate the challenges of interacting with life in the universe.

THE INTERVENTION is a dangerous form of contact underway by certain races from the Greater Community who are here to take advantage of a weak and divided humanity. This is occurring at a time when the human family is entering a period of increasing breakdown and disorder, in the face of the Great Waves of change. The Intervention presents itself as a benign and redeeming force while in reality its ultimate goal is to undermine human freedom and self-determination and take control of the world and its resources. The New Message reveals that the Intervention seeks to secretly establish its influence here in the minds and hearts of people at a time of growing confusion, conflict and vulnerability. God is calling us, as the native peoples of this world, to oppose this Intervention, to

THE POWER OF KNOWLEDGE

alert and educate others and to put forth our own rules of engagement as an emerging race. Our response to the Intervention and the Greater Community at large is the one thing that can unite a fractured and divided human family at a time of the greatest need and consequence for our race.

THE GREAT WAVES OF CHANGE are a set of powerful environmental, economic and social forces now converging in the world. The Great Waves are the result of humanity's misuse and overuse of the world, its resources and its environment. The Great Waves have the power to drastically alter the face of the world—producing economic instability, runaway climate change, violent weather and the loss of arable land and freshwater, threatening to produce a world condition of great difficulty and human suffering. The Great Waves are not an end times or apocalyptic event, but instead a challenging period of transition to a new world reality. The New Message reveals what is coming for the world and provides a preparation to enable us to navigate a radically changing world. God is calling for human unity and cooperation born now out of sheer necessity for the preservation and protection of human civilization. Together with the Intervention, the Great Waves represents one of the two great threats facing humanity and a major reason why God has spoken again.

HIGHER PURPOSE refers to the specific contribution each person was sent into the world to make and the unique relationships that will enable the fulfillment of this purpose. Knowledge within the individual holds their higher purpose and destiny for them, which cannot be ascertained by the intellect alone. These must be discovered, followed and expressed in service to others to be fully realized. The world needs the demonstration of this higher purpose from many more people as never before.

IMPORTANT TERMS

SPIRITUAL FAMILY refers to the small working groups formed after the Separation to enable all individuals to work towards greater states of union and relationship, undertaking this over a long span of time, culminating in their final return to God. Your Spiritual Family represents the relationships you have reclaimed through Knowledge during your long journey through Separation. Some members of your Spiritual Family are in the world and some are beyond the world. The Spiritual Families are a part of the mysterious Plan of God to free and reunite all those living in Separation.

ANCIENT HOME refers to the reality of life and the state of awareness and relationship you had before entering the world, and to which you will return after your life in the world. Your Ancient Home is a timeless state of connection and relationship with your Spiritual Family, The Assembly and God.

The Story of the Messenger

Marshall Vian Summers is the Messenger for the New Message from God. For over three decades he has been the recipient of a Divine Revelation given to prepare humanity for the great environmental, social and economic changes that are coming to the world and for humanity's contact with intelligent life in the universe.

In 1982, at the age of 33, Marshall Vian Summers was called into the deserts of the American Southwest where he had a direct encounter with the Angelic Presence, who had been guiding and preparing him for his future role and calling. This encounter forever altered the course of his life and initiated him into a deeper relationship with the Angelic Assembly, requiring that he surrender his life to God. This began the long, mysterious process of receiving God's New Message for humanity.

Following this mysterious initiation, he received the first revelations of the New Message from God. Over the decades since, a vast Revelation for humanity has unfolded, at times slowly and at times in great torrents. During these long years, he had to proceed with the support of only a few individuals, not knowing what this growing Revelation would mean and where it would ultimately lead.

The Messenger has walked a long and difficult road to receive and present the largest Revelation ever given to the human family. Still today the Voice of Revelation continues to speak through him as he faces the great challenge of bringing God's New Revelation to a troubled and conflicted world.

Read more about the life and story of the Messenger
Marshall Vian Summers:
www.newmessage.org/story-of-marshall-vian-summers

THE POWER OF KNOWLEDGE

Read and hear the original revelation *The Story of the Messenger:*
www.newmessage.org/story-of-the-messenger

Hear and watch the world teachings of the Messenger:
www.newmessage.org/messenger

THE VOICE OF REVELATION

For the first time in history, you can hear the Voice of Revelation, such a Voice as spoke to the prophets and Messengers of the past and is now speaking again through a new Messenger who is in the world today.

The Voice of Revelation is not the voice of one individual, but that of the entire Angelic Assembly speaking together, all as one. Here God communicates beyond words to the Angelic Assembly, who then translate God's Message into human words and language that we can comprehend.

The revelations of this book were originally spoken in this manner by the Voice of Revelation through the Messenger Marshall Vian Summers. This process of Divine Revelation has occurred since 1982. The Revelation continues to this day.

———— ✍ ————

Hear the original audio recordings of the
Voice of Revelation, which is the Source of the text contained
in this book and throughout the New Message:
www.newmessage.org/experience

Learn more about the Voice of Revelation,
what it is and how it speaks through the Messenger:
www.newmessage.org/voiceofrevelation

About The Society for the New Message from God

Founded in 1992 by Marshall Vian Summers, The Society for the New Message from God is an independent religious 501(c)(3) non-profit organization that is primarily supported by readers and students of the New Message, receiving no sponsorship or revenue from any government or religious organization.

The Society's mission is to bring the New Message from God to people everywhere so that humanity can find its common ground, preserve the Earth, protect human freedom and advance human civilization as we stand at the threshold of great change and a universe full of intelligent life.

Marshall Vian Summers and The Society have been given the immense responsibility of bringing the New Message into the world. The members of The Society are a small group of dedicated individuals who have committed themselves to fulfill this mission. For them, it is both a burden and a great blessing to give themselves wholeheartedly in this great service to humanity.

The Society for the New Message

Contact us:

P.O. Box 1724 Boulder, CO 80306-1724
(303) 938-8401 (800) 938-3891
011 303 938 84 01 (International)
(303) 938-1214 (fax)
society@newmessage.org
www.newmessage.org
www.marshallsummers.com
www.alliesofhumanity.org
www.newknowledgelibrary.org

THE POWER OF KNOWLEDGE

Connect with us:

www.youtube.com/thenewmessagefromgod
www.facebook.com/newmessagefromgod
www.facebook.com/marshallsummers
www.twitter.com/godsnewmessage

Donate to support The Society and join a community of givers who are helping bring the New Message to the world:
www.newmessage.org/donate

ABOUT THE WORLDWIDE COMMUNITY OF THE NEW MESSAGE FROM GOD

The New Message from God is being studied and practiced by people around the world. Representing more than 90 countries and studying the New Message in over 30 languages, a worldwide community of students has formed to both receive the New Message and support the Messenger in bringing God's New Message to the world.

The New Message has the power to awaken the sleeping brilliance in people everywhere and bring new inspiration and wisdom into the lives of people from all nations and faith traditions.

Learn more about the worldwide community of people who are learning and living the New Message and taking the Steps to Knowledge in their lives.

Read and hear the original Revelation *The Worldwide Community of God's New Message:*
www.newmessage.org/theworldwidecommunity

Join the free Worldwide Community site where you can meet other students and engage with the Messenger:
www.community.newmessage.org

Learn more about the educational opportunities available in the Worldwide Community:

Community Site - http://www.community.newmessage.org/
New Message Free School - www.community.newmessage.org/school
Live Internet Broadcasts and International Events -
www.newmessage.org/events

THE POWER OF KNOWLEDGE

Encampment - www.newmessage.org/encampment
Online Library of Text and Audio -
www.newmessage.org/experience

BOOKS OF THE NEW MESSAGE FROM GOD

God Has Spoken Again

The One God

The New Messenger

The Greater Community

The Journey to a New Life

Steps to Knowledge

Greater Community Spirituality

The Great Waves of Change

Life in the Universe

Wisdom from the Greater Community I & II

Secrets of Heaven

Relationships & Higher Purpose

Living The Way of Knowledge

CPSIA information can be obtained
at www.ICGtesting.com
Printed in the USA
FSHW020953310519
58507FS